# Journey of Angels:
## A Course in Life, Love and the Pursuit of Happiness

**Journey of Angels:**
A Course in Life, Love and the Pursuit of Happiness

By Danielle Fournier

King **W** Books  Seattle  2015

ISBN 978-0-692-44954-7

Published by King **W** Books

Seattle

For

my heroes
my villains
my friends

and my self that endured

God Bless You All

# Contents

# Preface

I am living proof you can change your life into what you always knew it could be.

Not long ago, I was $70,000 in debt, thirty pounds overweight, dating the wrong person (again) and angry, very angry.

Before that, I was 25 pounds overweight, in debt, afraid to fly, dating the wrong person, dreaming of seeing Paris one day.

Right before that, I was afraid to sing, 50 pounds overweight, and dropped out of high school because I had horrible panic attacks so acute I couldn't even ride in a car.

I dabbled in changing my life. I hoped, I wished. I dreamed. Then I hoped some more, dreamed some more. I gave up, started again, and then got discouraged. Eventually, I felt like life was wearing me down. I was approaching 40, alone and disparaged about the course of my life.

Worse yet, I was lost. I had given up on dreams, quit following through when it was hard, and settling for far below what I truly wanted or believed I deserved in life.

It didn't happen overnight. It might have, but I held on tight to the familiar. The harder I held on, the harder lessons I experienced trying to get me to let go. If I vowed to get rid of a problem but backed down when push came to shove, I quickly confronted the same monster- only twice as big, twice as ugly and much more smelly.

I decided to get out. Deep down, I knew I was meant for better. I lost sleep over it; I cried over it with my wine, I scribbled pages upon pages of my woes in journal upon journal. I studied, I read, and I grew. I would make a step forward, then back, but progress was made. Slowly, I awoke parts my true self, but then a catastrophe struck. Actually, three catastrophes happened.

My father got sick and died. My best friend dumped me. Then the new love of my life deserted ship. It was a catastrophic year. To top it off, I lived in a tiny apartment, couldn't pay my bills, and I woke up every day very unhappy.

I knew I could do better. I knew I was meant for more. I knew, deep in my heart, there was a plan for my life. I had a purpose.

But did I listen to that voice? Nope.

I decided to ignore it and began drinking. I turned off my feelings, tuned out my intuition, and then heaved everything mentally overboard.

For a month, I drank every day. I ate lots of sugar. I spent hours shopping travel on the Internet, spending money I didn't have, driving myself deeper into a financial hole. All I wanted was to stop feeling all those miserable feelings. My family feared for my life. I kept crying, sobbing uncontrollably and talking about killing myself.

Life didn't feel fair. Life felt hopeless. I just wanted the pain to stop.

I decided to run away. I lived in Seattle, a beautiful town of great trees and dynamic skies. It also has lots and lots of rain. I grew up in the high desert and I craved sunlight. So, I decided to head south to California, where I could paint, see a blue sky and figure out how it all went wrong.

The plan was to spend two months being creative. I was so confident I was going to "make it" that I gave notice at work. Thanks to an employer with his head about him, I got a sabbatical instead. Which was really good news, as it all turned out very differently than planned.

I packed up my apartment, gleefully posting on Facebook my plans to "find my happy". I sold my shoes (I had hundreds of pairs), went though one of three storage units and held garage sales. I packed three suitcases, my art studio, my guitar and my dog.

So long rain! See ya...never!

One week into my newfound life, I broke my foot. The break was so bad I needed surgery and a full time attendant. I had started seeing a friend from high school (far too soon) and he agreed to help me.

We had a ton of fun. We put on our swimsuits first thing every morning, made drinks and enjoyed relaxing.

Well, he enjoyed it. I went insane. I was here to find my happy! I was here to get famous, make a fortune, deliver a message of hope and peace, and become a great artist. Or something. I knew I was meant for something.

There is a saying, "Wherever you go, there you are."

This is never truer than when you want to find your mission in life. It is always inside you. I have literally been to 40 countries searching for "my thing". I have read hundreds of self-help books, taken class after class, and practiced most things short of voodoo trying to "figure it out".

Then it did. One day, it happened.

I found the secret that was holding me back. It was beautifully simple, yet ornate in the making. I had searched everywhere, yet it was always inside me. I just had to listen.

The gift of a crisis is that you find out what's important. Financially, medically, spiritually, mentally, emotionally, all crises point you to your truest self. And that's where you have to build a house, so to speak, on your solid spiritual foundation.

I found that no matter how many times I ignored that still, small voice inside of me, it never went away. That's what changed it all for me.

One night, after quite a few drinks and some serious despair, I hit my bottom. I knew I could do more with my life, but what? Why wasn't it working? What was wrong with me? I cried and cried.

Then I asked, "Please God, help me."

Quite clearly and suddenly, I heard that voice inside of me.

"Get a pen. Get some paper. Write this down."

I did. It flowed out, these thirty chapter titles that follow. It was clear this was the answer to what I needed to know about myself in order to change my life.

The next day, I sat down to write, very concerned that I was going crazy. How was I ever going to do this? As I started to write, a peace came over me. I was overwhelmed by a sense of beauty and peace. I truly feel that an angel entered my room and guided my writing. Every time I wrote, this happened.

As I wrote each day, my heart healed. I started laughing again. I found myself waking up saying, "Oh, I am so happy."

I believe this happened because I had not listened to my still, small voice for years. As I worked on the chapters, I not only wrote but also answered the questions for myself. My view of who I was, and why my life wasn't working, became pretty clear to me. I hadn't challenged my own thinking, nor did I give myself nearly enough credit for what I did so well in life. A gentle shift took place each day. I found peace. I found happiness. I found more love than I ever imagined was possible.

What's amazing to me is that it was always inside of me, just waiting for me to listen to that still, small voice.

You have it in you. You are blessed. You can do it. No one else can do what you do. You are beautiful, capable, and perfect in every way and you know it. Now it's time to live it.

To use this book, work through each chapter as it moves you. Some ideas will be difficult or challenging. Just stick with it and know that whatever area you find challenging needs your loving attention. Trust in the knowing that you are healing, from the inside out. Changes will come, some suddenly, some quietly, and some abruptly. Trust that your highest self is working right along with you to create deep, lasting peace and happiness.

It is recommended to read a chapter in the morning, and then do what it says to do. Don't skip the exercises! Some days you will cry when you read, your insides screaming, "that's me!" Some days you will "forget" to read until night instead of morning. Some days you will feel like it doesn't apply (it probably does) and the worst days you will throw this book across the room, righteously cursing it and shouting you can do better (maybe you can).

It's all true.

So, let's begin.

I did, and I was ready to end it all. Asking these questions of myself transformed my life with truth, love and peace. I pray it does the same for you.

Amen.


Danielle Fournier
La Quinta, CA 2015

# Just Quit

Say, "I quit."

Now yell, "I quit!"

Louder! I know you are still staying it in your head, but later, in your car, or on a beach- really do it. Say it loud. Say it proud. Because you really need to:

Quit the awful job. Quit the bad partner. Quit lying to yourself that you can't do better. Quit blaming the brownies for tempting you.

Quit saying you didn't "really" want to be an actor, a singer, a doctor, a race car driver, a vet, someone's lovely spouse, sail the world, buy that blouse, build the house, go to school, be more like Oprah, a beloved friend, someone people search out for advice, someone who changes the world for better.

Make a list, really fast. List five things you need to quit:
1.
2.
3.
4.

5.

Yes, smoking counts.

Yes, gossiping counts.

So does cheating on your taxes, eating "smaller" cartons of ice cream and being rude to the drive thru employees because you really hate your life.

You know what it is that you need to quit.

We all know what we need to quit; yet we continue. Chances are, there are 2-3 things that really hold you back- mine's sugar. I love to take the edge off my worries with some binge eating. It works, on a physical level. I get calmer. On a spiritual level, I die a little each time I cover up the thought that preceded it. I avoided fixing the problem, and created a new one with low self-esteem attached.

Another reason to quit is that there is something better coming for you. If you want outta your job, you might need a new one. Maybe the friend who is toxic takes all your focus off that nagging voice telling you to open your own business? Perhaps your endless interest in other people's problems covers up your feelings that your are not enough if you don't always "over help" totally capable people?

Quit now. Or the universe will make you quit later. Don't want to quit overeating sugar? How's diabetes look? Don't want to quit being addicted to stress? How do heart palpitations sound? Don't want to quit spending money you don't have because you are afraid your extra weight makes you unlovable so you buy hundreds of pairs of shoes? Try looking at seeing your home you bought at 25 foreclosed upon or selling it and moving to a tiny apartment where all you have left is shoes. Everything else you own is in storage because you no longer have credit to buy a home.

That last one was me. I couldn't face that my dwindling finances could no longer support my former lifestyle. Whatever you need to quit, it's your golden key to your success. That's why it's here first. Because we tell ourselves it's only _____. It's not, and you know it. Everything counts.

We tell ourselves so many untruths to avoid feeling scared, small, insecure and incapable. It's not true. It's all lies to stave off uncomfortable feelings we don't want to face. We fear the truth.  Never has the world seen so many brilliant, smart, creative, beautiful people. We live long lives. The question is, how will we live them? Angry, sad, depressed, or procrastinating for "someday?"

Or we can live them happy, day in, day out, knowing each footfall is taking us to our destiny, our truest self and a life built upon a bedrock of trust and self-esteem?

What do you need to quit? Say it now. Say it to yourself. Get professional help if you need it. Sometimes the bigger the challenge, the greater the destiny that awaits. You can do this.

The only thing you are not allowed to quit is yourself. You are too valuable to do that.

Write yourself a promise, tape it to your mirror or post it as a background on your phone. Date it. Sign it.

Here's what I need to quit:

You don't need to say when, where or how. You just need

to say it out loud to yourself. Your mind will do the rest for you. I promise.

Notes:

# Speak Wisely

Do you bless or curse people with that tongue of yours? Be honest. No one is looking.

Maybe a little of both, you say? How about yourself?

Are you, in fact, the meanest person in the world to yourself?

Do you regularly:

1. Tell yourself you are ugly, fat or dumb?
2. Tell other people the same thing about yourself?
3. Discourage your own dreams?
4. Shoot down your own ideas?
5. Talk yourself out of good ideas, one after the other?
6. Berate yourself for mistakes long gone by?
7. Relive the regrets of your day, every night as you lay in bed?
8. Tell other people about mistakes you make on a regular basis?
9. Wish you had done life differently?
10. Tell yourself it will never get better?

Any of these are poisons to your soul. Circle any of the above that you do to yourself.

Now, say this out loud:

"My future is before me. I am perfect, made by God and only the future matters."

Does it make you freak out to say this? Say it three more times.

This list is meant to create awareness. Don't be tempted to beat yourself up over any of these habits, for they are just that- habits.

Let's build some new ones. Pick three from the following list:

1. Dang, I am looking good today.
2. Dang, I am really good at _____ (kissing, smiling, laughing, etc.).
3. Dang, I am only 25, 35, 45, 55....that's (your age times 7) in dog years! I have a long way to go. Life ain't over yet.
4. The past is ancient history, put it in a book and shelve it.
5. The dream in my heart is real, that's why I have it.
6. The dream I have can happen, and I am the one to make it real.
7. Only I have my skills, my heart and my hope. I am the chosen one.
8. If I am truly at bottom, the only way out is up.
9. What if it does work?
10. What if I am the one?

How do you speak to others? Are you kind? Do you yell in traffic? Do you yell, period? Who do you really want to yell at?

List five people (including God) you would really like to yell at:

1.
2.
3.
4.
5.

Don't.

Do something much better. Next to each person's name, write **Forget** or **Forgive**.

On the **Forgive** list:

Be honest with yourself. You do not have to say it aloud, but you need to do it inside.
Anger only makes you miserable, and it taints every relationship you have. Some of you may have "me" in the people you'd like to yell at. That's OK. However, yelling solves nothing unless you need help when you are stranded in a forest. In many cases, it makes a situation worse. Forgive your family, yourself, your exes, the people who undoubtedly did you wrong. Everyone who ever insulted you, made you feel weak, broke your heart, led you astray.

They made you stronger. You are still here. They never won. You are a champion.

On your **Forget** list:

You need closure with these people.

Write them a thank you note. They made you stronger. You are still here. They never won. You are a champion. Scars heal, unless you pick the scab, then they take much longer. You have beautiful things to do here on planet earth, and happiness is the best revenge.

Now is the time to take the lessons of any one or anything that makes you angry.

What about dumb people, bad drivers, rude people, you say?

This is on your **Forget** list as well. Are you really going to let a bad driver ruin your life? Will you give them that power? Worse yet, if you commute for hours each day, chances you are ruining several hours each day as you head somewhere important. On your way to work, you arrive mad when you should be concentrating on your bread and butter. On your way home, you arrive mad to greet the people who mean the most to you.

Need to be vengeful? Smile at people who cut you off! Wave. Cheerfully!   That will totally throw them off balance. You can be nice when someone is a jerk. It starts with you. Break the chain of rude. Start a nice revolution.

A special note to people who "hate stupid people": it's about you, not them. You are being mean to yourself. Chances are, you have failed yourself in some way, and you are taking it out on others. Be honest. Why are you so mad? Children are not as "smart" as you. Neither are animals. You are nice to them, I bet. If you are not, revisit your names list. And let go. They never ruined your soul. You are okay, beautiful just as you are. Honor that by moving on and speaking peace.

Mad at the government? Step up! Run for office.

Want to yell at the president? Write a thoughtful letter.

Think long and hard before you send it. Better yet, vote next election.

Want to yell at people who use plastic and send it out to the sea to create the great Pacific garbage gyre? Start a non-profit, get involved, use other materials and educate people.

Yelling, at yourself or others, rarely creates the results you want. Many times it does the opposite.

Maybe you need to start singing or embark on a speaking career. Do you love yelling at your television during the games? What about becoming a referee? Talk back to the newscast? Politics might be for you, or activism.

List five ways you could use that voice for something constructive:
1.
2.
3.
4.
5.

If you mostly target yourself, list three things you need to change right now:
1.
2.
3.

These are most likely the reasons you are angry at yourself. Be gentle. Do they have a root cause, a common thread? Is it your voice or someone else's?

Examples:

1. I hate you! You are lazy.
2. You always screw up.
3. You are so fat.
4. You never finish anything.
5. No one will ever love us/me/you.
6. It's over. I can't go on.

My child, my darling, first, let me say it's okay. It really is. It can be healed. It can be fixed. You are not broken, although you may really feel that way.

If number 6 is one of your statements, you may need some professional help, a great friend, or some clergy to talk to. You may have been through an earthly version of hell, but you can recover. It's not over; you can rebound. If you are still alive, the world has a use for you. Your journey, your purpose, is not yet finished.

If you are feeling like it's over- get help. Tell someone, anyone! It brings daylight in. You can't quit, my friend. Chances are, you just want to end the pain because you know it can be better but you don't know how. Talk to someone. Call a hotline, call a therapist, walk into an ER if you have to. Don't quit.

Let go of speaking anger now, because you have much better things to do with your life.

Start today.

Write out a statement, a letter, a sentence, whatever you need to heal to each of the five names on your list. Pour it all out. Every last bit. Leave nothing out. You can burn this if you want afterwards.

For each **Forgive** name, write I forgive you after the entry.

For each **Forget** name, write Goodbye after the entry.

Take one more action with your list. Burn it. Buy it dinner. Mail it to Santa Claus for the naughty list (or, stretch like the Grinch and hope for a nice list). Throw it in a body of water (paper, please). Just get rid of it in a blaze of glory.

You never are going to yell at those people again, especially that beautiful soul in the mirror.

Amen.

Notes:

# You Are Not Your Past

Leave yesterday where it was meant to stay, all alone in the past. Of course, you can learn from your mistakes, but don't live in yesterday. Whatever mistakes you made, it doesn't really matter in terms of how your future turns out. You can overcome all of it.

How old do you have to be to really think about not going to college if you want to? About four years from dying, I'd say. At age 65, most states have schools that offer tuition waivers? A college degree for nearly free! Beats the heck out of student loans.

Did you know that in classical singing, most singers aren't taken seriously in their twenties or thirties?

Have you ever thought your age might help not be a hindrance? What if your age is the thing that sells your talent? You could be a phenomenon waiting to happen.

Ok, so maybe you failed at many businesses (I myself had three big flops). Did you learn what not to do? Maybe you had three, four, or five marriages. Have you learned from that experience? Maybe now you at least know what love is not. Maybe you realize you need to hit the road and be a wanderer. Not everyone is great at marriage.

What if you have screwed up one thing after another? Business, relationship, friendship, gained more weight instead of losing it? So what? Respectfully, I say, so what?! That's no reason to quit.

Look at batting averages. Baseball legends only hit the ball a third of the time. Remember, all the successes you know people for say nothing about how many times they failed getting to the top.

What's your worst failure?

Can you redo it? Do you really want to?

If you can make amends, do it now. Pick up the phone, write the letter, pay the bill.

Otherwise, write down ten things you learned from your worst failure:
1.
2.
3.
4.
5.
5.
7.
8.
9.
10.

Circle three that have served you since then. Do you see

how you grew?

Name the single most valuable lesson in your failure:


Now choose three things you never want to experience again:
1.
2.
3.

What steps could you take to never have it happen again?
1.
2.
3.

Hint: If it is never fail, fall in love or care, start over. These are not realistic goals. You will fail at something, you will care again and you will most likely love again. That is, if you wish to remain human.

Now, what are you holding onto that you should let go of?

If fear of pain comes up, that's normal. No one wants to suffer, feel sad, feel defeated or give up a dream. Sometimes you may have let go of something in the past to begin a new dream. One door closes so one can open.

Name three times an ending was really a beginning:
1.
2.
3.

How did you feel when they ended? How long did a new beginning take? Was it worth it?

Do you feel like you are marked somehow by a past event? Do you feel scarred or battered and bruised beyond repair?

Maybe it's so awful you can't say it aloud. That's okay.

Examples:

1. I don't trust.
2. I hate men/women/dogs/cars/planes/disco music.
3. My soul is broken, scarred and beyond repair.

Name three habits you created in the wake of the event that have made your life different now:

1.
2.
3.

Your pain is real, I will tell you that. But it does not need to be permanent. It may feel awful, irreparable and life altering.

I am here to tell you it is what you say it is. Your soul is indestructible. Whether you believe it is matter or energy that cannot be destroyed or if you believe it is the providence of God, you cannot ever be changed from your true nature.

You are a child of the universe. You cannot lose.

Nelson Mandela spent years in prison, but went on to lead a nation. You don't need to do anything to be restored, except say it.

Go to a mirror and say this. Brace yourself.

I am fine. I am perfect. Nothing was ever taken from me. I

am a most high child of God (Universe/Divine/etc.). I am still perfect, just the way I am.

Say it again. Say it three or four times every day. It may feel uncomfortable or untrue.

Write it down. Stick it in your wallet, in the visor of your car, in your underwear drawer or boldly place it on your refrigerator. Whatever you do, start repeating it every day.

Because the truth is, you are whole. You are beautiful and you have a place in this world filled with love.

Notes:

# Find Beauty

Lo, behold the light breaking.

When was the last time you saw a sunrise? What color is your daughter's hair? What's your favorite sight on your way to work? What moves you to tears?

Beauty is not just something we put on. Beauty is found on the inside, but it resides in you, not others. You will never see beauty anywhere if you cannot see it in yourself first.

What inspires you?

It is colors? Music? Textures? Shape? Movement? Are you spellbound by mathematics, relationship or deduction?

Perhaps you already know what kind of learner you are. Perhaps you have been trying too force yourself to experience the world in a way that does not suit you.

Do you love bubble baths and should choose that to try to unwind over TV?

Do you love a raucous tumble with your kids or a wild game of catch with your pets?

Do you prefer quiet or silence and a slow, steady breathing exercise while your mind unfurls from the day?

Maybe you love to draw or play music. Maybe cooking relaxes you.

Do you love games, puzzles, or reading?

Or maybe you need a brawling game of basketball with friends?

List five things that inspire you:
1.
2.
3.
4.
5.

List five things that relax you:
1.
2.
3.
4.
5.

Look at your lists. Each activity is centered on a certain type of learning. After each entry, write V for visual, F for feeling, H for hearing, P for physical, M for mental.

This may seem like it has nothing to do with finding beauty, but it does. This will show you how you learn, how you process information and how you process your surroundings.

This is where one man's beauty can be another man's

eyesore. Or it can be your spouse's biggest gripe. And the reason you can find beauty in your life is because you see it where you need to see it.

For example, a visual person can easily find inspiration in seascapes, art galleries or a well appointed home. A hearing inclined person may find it hard to relax without quiet or sound of their making (their choice of music, birdsong, or movie soundtrack). A feeling person needs sensuality, inner peace and perhaps ultra soft sheets. Without some form of outlet like sports (including sex), a physical person can get cranky. A cerebral person will crave great conversation or perhaps a good book to relax.

To find your own sense of beauty in this world, you must know where to look. One man's treasure is another woman's worn out recliner! Just because you see the beauty in a crooked tree or the graceful curl of your house's trim paint, doesn't mean anyone else will.

Beauty is personal. This is so evident when we look at possible mates. We all have known a friend who raves about their new love, only to be presented with our own version of a troll. By no means am I saying anyone is ever a troll, but there's no denying some prefer blonde to brunette, nearly faint for redheads or will be tongue tied at an accent while left uninspired by your own version of George Clooney.

Let's apply this to where you live. Do you live somewhere that inspires you? Is your home the way you want it? Is it noisy? Do you like/trust your neighbors? Is your place the center of the known universe for a three-block radius or do you wish you could cast a cloaking spell over it?

Look around your home, be it ever so humble, and find three things you really, really dig:

1.
2.
3.

Now find three things you really want to change:
1.
2.
3.

Does the pretty light from the window outweigh the nasty neighbor upstairs? Does your cat tell other cats he's really just visiting because you have heaps of laundry undone in your hallway? Or is this your dream house, filled with people you love?

Start noticing the little things that make you smile. A bird you watch, the way your daughter eats every third Cheerio, the sunlight across your walls, the sound of your family getting ready for the day- these are the clues that show you how you find beauty in this world.

Finding what's beautiful is the cure for "what's wrong" with life. Find a thousand tiny reasons to smile, be inspired, and let love through each day. If you have trouble finding beautiful moments, make a list as you go through the day.

If you are having a really tough time in your life, start really small. As my Dad died of cancer, some days all I could find to start my list were simple things like: my pen has ink. We still have milk left (yea, no store!) The grass is growing. I like my fingernails. I am still alive.

Eventually, you will begin to notice more and more things of beauty in your world.

For example, you could find yourself saying things like:

Wow, the store clerk has a great smile. Wow, my car is actually really fast, who needs all four fenders? Wow, my hair is fabulous, the stylist is right. Wow, I never noticed that great tree at the intersection before. Wow, my office really has a great view. Wow, my uniform actually is a great color for my skin. Wow, my parents really taught me to make a killer pancake.

You don't have to be famous, rich or influential to be happy. In fact, you won't be happy with any of those things if you are not happy first. It will just be you, only with different outside circumstances. (Think of all those celebs who are unhappy- that could be you.) It's the inside that must shift, no matter where you are.

Find the beauty in yourself. What are you good at that no one could ever steal? Do you have a great sense of humor? Are you fast? Are you kind? Are you patient, clever, soft, gentle, thoughtful, happy, dreamy, helpful, creative?

Your number one quality is:


Start applying that to your drive, your work, your friends, or your relationships. This is your beauty. Paint it all over town.

Notes:

# Who Are You To Judge?

Now, about love… Let's talk about love.

What kind of love?

Who do you love? What do you love? What loves you back?

What is love? We all think we know what the word means. But what is love in action?

What are you willing to do or be to have the things you love, or the people?

To love is not to simply want something or someone. To love something we must first accept it into ourselves. We must make it part of us, and we a part of it.

When we love people, we admire traits about them, be it their smile, their eyes, their wit, their kindness. Whatever allures us to a person, love walks in when we are faced with the beauty of their soul.

This is very natural to us as people. This is what happens

when we instantly fall in love with children, animals or a place. Its inner sanctum is exposed so genuinely, we can't help but see the truth residing there. What stops us with other adults is that we are caught up in exposing them under the cover of their culture; only we look to disrobe them of the very wrong thing. We seek to understand people from a level of mind, not the level of heart.

Have you ever had a conversation with a person who cannot speak your language, but know exactly what's happening? Have you ever looked into the eyes of an animal and saw understanding? Have you told someone you love them with your eyes? Have you ever been healed by a touch, had a hug that fixed all the day's sorrows or brought someone to tears with the touch of your hand?

This is pure love, pure acceptance, pure understanding. Your soul is touching theirs, ever so gently. This is so powerful, we can't understand what full integration with our souls would mean. We would be back on the other side!

Leadership author Stephen Covey said, "Love is a verb." It is not just a thing. It is an act, a willing act, to acknowledge the soul of another in its perfect glory. This is also why love can hurt so deeply. Once you have seen the beauty of that soul, not only is it hard to let it go, it is hard to see it suffer. Think of the pain of seeing a loved one in illness, in heartbreak, in hardship. It's far worse than the pain of separation or simply missing them.

When we do not acknowledge the beauty of another under the culture of our different learned personalities, traits and actions, we succumb to a numbness that betrays who we really are. This numbness makes violence, anger, war, selfishness, and ambivalence possible because we see not a soul, nor even sometimes a person, but a collection of thoughts, representations and ideologies that may or may not look anything like us.

Living on earth, it is very easy to justify getting mad in traffic, mad at the television, mad in the supermarket. On one hand, we know they are just like us on a soul level so we get frustrated we can't connect. On the other hand, we use our brains to rationalize why we cannot.

For example, you try to make friendly talk to a checker who is so busy she has left her pen in her ear and is searching for it through each order, clueless to its position. She barely acknowledges your "hello", practically throws your eggs into a bag and yells for a drawer count while telling you your total. You feel slighted/offended/insignificant as you punch in your PIN to give up your hard earned money (to this person). You now understand the need for automated checkouts and in fact welcome them as you have now justified your own logic. Later, you will tell your friends/spouse/kids how checkers are rude, people are rude, or the world is rude.

Stop for a moment. What if you had truly tried to connect? How would you do it?

Strangers have become frightening people in this world, a fate yet to be determined. What if they are just scared, lonely, insecure or bored like you? What if that checker can't pay her rent? What if her husband is cheating on her and she suspects? What if you look like the person who taunted her in high school? What if her father is dying? What if she simply was shy?

What does your face say when you go about life? What are you bringing to the table? Are you sweet, friendly, kind, and articulate? If you are shy, can you just tell people right off? If you are introverted, can you say, "I love you, but I need my space right now, be back soon!" with your eyes?

Think about John F Kennedy's famous question in terms of relationships. Ask not what you are getting from your interactions, but what are you giving? Are you a good listener, not forming questions while someone is speaking? Do you even wait for them to finish? Ask yourself what you want from the exchange that you are not getting.

The only right answer is connection.

Here are all the wrong answers: politeness, "respect", admiration, authority, bowing, favor, worship, acceptance, permission, or approval. These all stem from a deeper need to connect, to share, to acknowledge the soul. It's another being like you, for Heaven's sake! Of course you want to say, "Hi, how's earth treating you?"

This is why chance encounters can be so meaningful. We get to recognize the beauty, the love, the soul in others, even strangers. In our hearts, we all know we are here alone, albeit somehow together. Don't believe me? Try getting into someone else's head, even someone you know well like a spouse or a sibling. They will surprise you, even forty years down the line.

It's no surprise we are disappointed with people. We know we are all made of the same stuff. Many animal lovers are so passionate about them over people because animals offer simple, straightforward exchanges. You pet them, they purr, wag or snort. Have you ever wanted to go hug a stranger? Did you not do it because of how you were afraid of how they would react, not because of how you felt about it?

This is love, unadulterated. Love is action. The simple moment of feeling connection and taking it into your heart, that's love. It's so simple and we make it hard on ourselves.

Consider someone in your life you "love, but can't stand".

What do you love about them?

Why can't you stand them?

They don't listen- lack of connection. They talk over you- lack of connection. You come from different worlds? You see potential in them that they do not live up to. You see beauty in them they do not acknowledge. You see how talented, beautiful, funny, smart, loyal they would be if only they would...

This is lack of connection, love that wants to express itself but cannot find a place to land. So you get frustrated and give up. You love from afar, hoping for those rare moments when you can see eye to eye.

Start practicing love. Focus on what you are bringing, not getting. Connection will happen much more often.

What have you got to lose?

Notes:

# Get Gratitude, Now!

Why not be thankful for the stars above?

Do they not shelter you, guide you across the seas, fill your imagination?

Sometimes it may seem very hard to be thankful for things you cannot see- like grace, mercy, love, guidance or integrity, but how about saying thanks for your everyday life?

Make a quick list of three things you can't live without:
1.
2.
3.

Now say thank you for _____ because it _____.

Example:

Thank you for the trees because they are so beautiful, give me shelter and keep the rain off my head.

You now have gratitude list. Ta da! See how easy it is?

There's always something to be grateful for, no matter what your circumstances may be.    The great thing about gratitude is that it points your compass north. It is very difficult to be discouraged, upset, or unhappy and feel grateful at the same time. Yes, it's true that sometimes our lives are difficult and feel like nothing is going right. Chances are, even on our darkest days, something is right. Maybe it's the sun shining, the smell of hot coffee or simply the joy of tuning out the world to your favorite music. Whatever is getting you down, a good dose of gratitude can alleviate or lessen painful thoughts.

If you are in the midst of a large difficulty, a divorce, the death of a loved one, bankruptcy, or illness, it can seem nearly impossible to find a silver lining to the cloud. Gratitude can help you get though even the toughest time. Believe it or not, there are thanks to be found in the direst times.

List five things that could be good about your bad situation:
1.
2.
3.
4.
5.

If you had to, could something here help you grow? Bring you joy? Make you laugh?

Look at a former situation that you thought was difficult. List three things that happened as a result or that you learned from it:
1.
2.
3.

Perhaps life is going your way. You are swinging on the moon and dancing near the stars. Have you said thank you yet? Are you grateful to the people who helped you along the way? Is there someone you need to say thank you to but haven't done so? Are you forgetting to thank the little guy, your best friend or even your spouse?

List five people who got you where you are today:
1.
2.
3.
4.
5.

Feel like no one has ever helped you out? That's unlikely as it is impossible to get through this world alone. Think about people who have helped you grow, stretch, cared for you, made you laugh, made you comfortable, inspired you or taught you something.

List three people from age 0-10 that helped you grow up:
1.
2.
3.

List three people who helped you from age 10-20:
1.
2.
3.

List another three people who helped you from age 20-30:
1.
2.
3.

For each additional decade up to your age, list three more

people who have helped you.

It's a pretty impressive list, isn't it? Is there someone there you really need to email or send a letter to? The fourth grade teacher who fostered your love of reading? The coach who pushed you to excel beyond your limits? The lender who believed in your dream? How about the barista who greets you every morning with a smile, even though she's been up for hours before you? What about the aunt who made you sit up straight, so now you have nice posture?

Sometimes, we forget that we "get" to do something versus we "have" to do something. Really, we get to clean our home, go to work, get some exercise or do our studies. If you were homeless, wouldn't you envy mowing grass or cleaning windows? Would you happily do laundry or sing as you did dishes if you were faced with an eviction? Think about the first time you moved out on your own. It was a thrill to move furniture, shop for groceries and pay bills. If you can't pay your bills, focus on the ones you can pay. If you can't pay any of them, give thanks for things that are free (sunlight, parks, food samples or demonstrations, foods you can gather or hunt). I am not making light of any situation, but you can. The beauty of this world is that change is ever coming, and you can use that to your advantage! This, too, shall pass.

List five free things you can be grateful for:
1.
2.
3.
4.
5.

Now list five things you have received for free in the past month (free samples count!):

1.
2.
3.
4.
5.

Say thank you after each one, with all your heart.

Are you beginning to notice how much comes to you? Sometimes it feels as if we are chasing our destinies, but really they are rising up to meet us. They give back to us and support us all along the way, if only we are willing to look for how they are doing so.

Starting tomorrow morning, make a list of ten things you are grateful for each morning. Buy a journal, speak to text or email into a device, or type it out. It will only take a few moments, but as the pages accumulate, you will see how much goodness there really is in your life! It's everywhere; we must only pay attention to how much we are really receiving.

Notes:

# Truth Is Relative. So Is Pain.

The worst thing that has happened to you is completely real- for you.

With complete respect, I say it is indeed the worst thing you have lived through. Someone else's Something Awful may or not be better or worse. Some people go through hell on earth in this life, while others escape with relatively minor problems. Maybe it's not fair, to the outsider, but really, you don't know their pain.  It may be a break up, an illness, not achieving their potential, an injury, an unfair situation or a perceived failure- it's all relative. The worst thing, the tragedy, is simply the worst pain they have had to encounter in their lives.

We have all encountered an article in the news where we read of someone triumphing over horrible diseases, abject poverty, a learning disability, or an addiction to rise to great heights. Sometimes, that great height is simply a spinal cord injury taking a first step- something many people take for granted every day.

Perhaps you think that what you are going through, no one can understand. You are right, on one level. The scar you have from not getting a place on the track team might mean nothing to someone who isn't athletic. Likewise, you may not be able to see why surviving spouses struggle to stay alive when their partner passes, especially if you are unmarried or especially independent. Some people overcome their past, their tough childhoods, their mistakes, using the experiences to grow, or to draw upon for their art, or to set an example of how it will not be passed to another generation. Others are battle scarred and enduring the pain everyday. You cannot always tell what someone's Something Awful is.

The point is, you are carrying around your Something Awful. So is everyone else. By understanding that it is the worst thing in their life, past or present, you create grounds for compassion. For example, it is popular today to dismiss any problem of luxury as a "first world" problem, when, in fact, few people have real experience to compare that problem to. This is unfortunate because it causes a rift in real understanding. How would one expect to create water supplies in foreign countries if all you have ever done is turn on a tap? If it fails, you have the luxury of calling a plumber, a friend, or searching the Internet for information. It may very well create a crisis for you or your town if the water remains off for extended periods of time. You, your family, and your community, need water for drinking, hygiene, and food production. At the very least, it downgrades your standard of living for a while. This could very well be the worst problem of your week or month.

If you lived in a place, say, parts of Africa, where there was no tap, no well, no city water, no county irrigation, no federal program to bring each person water, could you so easily dismiss the problem? But perhaps the wife suffering HIV in Africa isn't so distressed she must walk for water, as she relishes the fresh air in comparison to her steel roofed shack. Maybe she takes heart in talking to others at the well or river, where she can listen and learn about the day's events. She is thankful the river is running at all this year. Last year it did not. Today she is not thinking about the river, but about whether or not she will live long enough to give birth to the child she is carrying.

Can you see how both of these could completely occupy your mind as Something Awful? You are both right. You may feel it is unfair to compare a woman dying with a person out of water, but it is an illustration to us how we are viewing the world from out own perspective. We do this every day. We do not take the time to consider what another person may be facing in their lives. We are quick to condemn them, write them off, and dismiss them as foolhardy, rude, lazy or stupid.

Think about your Something Awful. Sit with it for a moment.

Can you fix it? Change it? Work with it? Let it inspire you to greatness?

Be very honest with yourself, can most people relate to your pain (a divorce, debt, unfairness, alienation, illness etc.)? Or do you have a special wound, something you feel makes you feel so different form people (concentration camp experience, sexual or physical abuse, childhood warfare, multiple deaths of loved ones, mental or terminal illness)?

This is not to compare pain, but to realize exactly the opposite. Just as you cannot taste someone else's food, you cannot feel their pain. They also cannot feel yours, especially when this is an unusual circumstance. If you feel alienated because you feel your problem is unique, that makes sense. How do you tell someone about the horror of spending your childhood in institutions or orphanages or seeing your loved one die in front of you?

We have to let go of the expectation that people will feel our pain. They can't. Sometimes they don't want to. Should they have to? This is at once an argument for compassion and an opportunity to reduce our expectations of others. We can gain compassion for others by trying to see their pain, knowing we might fail completely. For instance, can you imagine the pain of losing a child? It's difficult to fathom, even more if you do not have children of your own. This in no way makes you less compassionate; it makes you human. Realize this as a limitation and make an effort to expand your sense of empathy. The person is hurting, and that is really all that matters.

Think about your Something Awful(s). List them here.
1.
2.
3.

Think about someone close to you. List their Something Awful:

How does it affect their life, past, present and future?

Think about the worst things that ever happened to your parents. Can you list them?

Think about the worst things that ever happened to your grandparents. Can you list them?

How does/did it affect their life, past, present and future?

Here's the kicker. Holding onto your Something Awful can hold you back from happiness. If you relive that something everyday, every hour, you are dwelling there. This is very common, yet very destructive. The meaning you give the event frames how you see its impact in your life.  Do you think it helped you grow? Do you think it has hampered you? How did you decide?

List how your worst thing helped your life:

List how it hurt it:

Can you change that pain into power somehow? What lesson could you learn? Does it make a great story? Does it serve as an excuse to not do something you are afraid of doing? Can others see something you cannot? Are you willing to consider a different answer to what it might mean in your life or to others? Are you willing to consider seeing past people's behavior? Their worst pain, by far, is their worst pain. As is yours.

So, what's the truth?

# Expect More

You deserve so much more.

No matter where you are in this life. You deserve more. More love, more happiness, more peace, more prosperity.

What do you expect out of your life? Do you expect to simply get by, hoping to catch up next month? Do you dream of moving to a new home, yet not actually believe it will ever happen? Do you expect good things to happen to you, or do you brace each moment for the tragic? Has hope died in your life? Have you quit dreaming, just so you won't be disappointed?

Are you only settling for scraps, when you once dreamed of so much more? Do you limit yourself by saying it can never happen?

What if it did? Who would you be then?

Make a list of things you have given up on ever getting in this life:
1.
2.
3.
4.

5.

After each entry, write why you have given up on it.

Can you change any of your entries? For example, if you decided something was "too hard", could you make it easier by taking small steps, getting support from friends or relatives, or getting advice? Write yes, no, or maybe next to each entry.

How do you cheat or cheapen yourself? Think about all the things you do that make you feel rich, well cared for and successful? (For some of you, none may be the answer.) These are the little things that spell success to you, signals to you that you are doing pretty well.

List three things that make you feel rich:
1.
2.
3.

Now list three things that make you feel cheap/cheated:
1.
2.
3.

Is there some way you can eliminate the cheap/cheated list? For example, could you window-shop your dream store once a month instead of binge discount shopping every week? Make a statement to expect more from you life.

No matter where you come from, chances are you can only imagine so much goodness in your life. You have established boundaries in your mind as to how far you can soar. For one person, it could be the idea of leaving the state, another leaving the country, still another leaving civilization for a camel ride across Namibia.

If you can't conceive it, you cannot achieve it. Your mind will say, "I can't even imagine living there." Or "I can't imagine that much freedom", or "I can't imagine all that extra money. Whatever would I do with myself?"

Imagine a genie would grant you your three deepest wishes. What would you wish for?

1.
2.
3.

The life you are seeking is seeking you as well. Don't be afraid to dream big, because you really do anyway. We all have big dreams in our hearts, but we are afraid to let them out. We are afraid to hope, to care, to commit. However, when we quit hoping, we stop growing. If there is not something pulling us forward, we are apt to wander. Sometimes wandering is great. Sometimes wandering gets us lost, aimless, or adrift. Without hope, we stagnate. Imagine your hope is a compass pointing north. Constantly expanding your vision will enlarge your map. Hope drives the way.

Dream up something sexy. Do you want a car or a special person? How about a lavish house or one to give to your Mom? What is it you dare not hope for? World peace? Do you want to feed hungry children or bring water to a village in a different nation? Would you like to make art that touches people? How about making more friends? How about learning a language- in its country of origin?

List five things that seem outlandish to want.

1.
2.

3.
4.
5.

Choose one you believe you can actually get. Now list three steps you can take this week to make it start happening:
1.
2.
3.

Now choose one that seems impossible:


Has anyone ever done this? Can you copy their success to achieve the same results? Can you read a book, take a course, serve as an apprentice, "fake it until you make it", or find a person to believe in you?

If the thing you are dreaming of has never been done, can you read about pioneers in their fields? Many were once outcasts, felt alienated or scoffed at before their ideas changed history.

List three people who could become your heroes:
1.
2.
3.

Read up on them. Are they similar to you? Did they almost give up? Did they believe when no one else did? Who were their heroes? Why didn't they give up? How are they different than other people?

Now it's time for conquering the objections. We all have excuses/reasons we cannot accomplish our dreams. Some seem very valid, while others we can readily see through ourselves. They all stem from the same place, fear. It's OK to feel the fear, but it is best to go ahead and do it anyway. If we are unhappy with the direction of our lives, we can begin planning anew by asking ourselves what we really want.

What I really want:
1.
2.
3.
4.
5.

What I settle for:
1.
2.
3.
4.
5.

Are you afraid you don't deserve it? The truth is, maybe none of us deserve anything. Maybe we really do get what we expect, what we hope for, what we are willing to want. Most times, we wish to get by, but feel like asking for more is selfish or arrogant. Perhaps you feel cannot ask for more when someone has less. Instead, ask yourself how you might help them if you had more. Would it be enough? Or would you love to give them their deepest wish? What if we were living in a world where people were all giving each other their best? How can it ever start if it doesn't start with one person?

You could be the person who dares to get out of poverty, go to college, or start a business in your community. Your dream could ignite thousands more. Don't be afraid to hope, as it will only come to pass if you believe it can happen.

Nobody else. You have to believe.

Become a blessing to others. Start by blessing yourself.

# Burn, Baby, Burn

Passion is the only thing that matters. Your passion is what fuels your movement in this world. If you are not excited everyday, you are not living in your passion. Worlds collide and are changed by passion. Passion is another name for our inner fire. Its definition can be elusive, but like art, you know it when you see it. What ignites our drive in this world isn't the same for all of us. What's important is that you know what drives you.

You may be a very calm person. You may value order, reserve and patience above all else, but that does not mean you are not deeply enthralled by your passion. Passion is something that can be recognized by a glow in the eyes, a certain set of the chin, a dogged determination to see it through to its end, even if that end is years away.

Of course, you may be a person who is a fiery trailblazer, a rainmaker, a leader who claims the room with a booming voice and carriage of being. People often say you have great passion, are a firebrand or a natural leader. This is a more obvious kind of passion that we often refer to when we people living their passion.

The truth is, passion does not need to speak loudly. Consider monks. Not often do you see bombastic monks speaking loudly (if at all), but can you question their devotion to their cause? Passion is spirit applied to life. Think of Yo-Yo Ma, soft-spoken cellist of international renown. His bow sets the instrument afire when he plays, yet he does it in his quiet own way.

Passion directs your course in life. When we seize upon our passion (which may be our family, our church, out creativity, our need to help others, or any number of driving forces), we tap into our greatest source of fuel. It is a unique force that drives us to a new place while ensuring we never stay still for long. Passion applied to daily living makes us wildly optimistic about our lives, day in and day out. Without it, we stagnate, feel dull or lifeless and can become depressed.

What do you desire? What moves you? Do you know the answers to these questions?

List five things you are passionate about:
1.
2.
3.
4.
5.

Do these things have an element in common? Like beauty, compassion, creativity, structure, responsibility, exploration, etc.? Let's call this your theme. For example, a person who loves painting, poetry, cooking and sewing could describe all of those activities as creative or artistic. It could be broader like home or art. A person who loves gardening, singing, shopping and children could choose connection or teaching or interacting. Think broadly on this choice because it defines your passion its greatest arc. This is the overall theme that is most important to you, which leads you to your interests. There is nothing wrong with your interests as your greatest passion, but what would happen if you, Heaven forbid, could not do that certain thing any more?

If you were a painter and could no longer see, what might you choose to pursue? This may be unkind, but the reality is, sometimes we cannot pursue our greatest interest for one reason or another. I am not saying you should ever quit, but if you loved to paint but loved to sing more, and someone offered you a chance to become a famous painter, could you step forward gratefully and let your other interests take front stage? This is not the same as giving up on your dreams, but much more like what we do everyday to make ends meet. We trade some of our biggest dreams for our other talents in the name of our greater goal and gifts.

Sometimes we are happy, sometimes not. Every day may not be perfect. They key is to determine when you are within your passion realm and when you are simply good at something, but find little or no joy in its performance. Perhaps you are a good salesperson, but your introverted nature makes it very difficult for you to interact all day long. You no longer want to paint, talk to your spouse, or even play with the dog when you arrive at home. Your skills as a friendly, responsible, well-trained employee who loves what you sell makes you one of your boss's favorites, but you practically hate what you do every day. You are tired, cranky and burning (or burned) out, even though you are good at it. This is not in your passion realm!

Returning to our idea of theme, what guides your life? Animals? The outdoors? Progress? Technology? People? Service? Spirituality? Love?

If you created a non-profit, whom would it be for?

These are your "people". How do you want to help them?

1.
2.
3.
4.
5.

List five things you do to help them now.

1.
2.
3.
4.
5.

Is this your job? Or not even close to it? Do you use your job to fund what you are passionate about? Could you combine your talents to make a new opportunity for yourself? It is my firm belief people are here to advance the world, each one blessed with gifts that serve their soul's mission in this life. Your gifts point to your mission.

For some, this requires a little digging to discern their passion, because it can looks like a tool box full of skills but no project to work on. You don't know if you like cars or motorcycles or if you should be working on a ski lift with this beautiful shiny wrench you have. That's totally fine. Not everyone is the rock star, which is great because someone needs to be a chef, a teacher, a banker who gives people a second chance, a neighbor who everyone can count on. It's not about your job title; it's about your passion to serve your purpose.

If you notice in your daily life what gets you excited, what keeps you inspired, you will begin to see your passion lying underneath it all. Now is the chance to begin doing more of those things in your everyday life. The more passionate you are about your life, the better you life will feel. Passion creates drive, energy, happiness and fulfillment.

It can be tough when you see your passion, feel it deep into your bones, pursue it with your whole heart but it seems to be going nowhere. The key is to live one day at a time. Because, even when you do "make it", that's exactly what you will do then. If you are an artist, you are going to do that art each day, maybe even more than you thought. Will you still love it? Or are you chasing the challenge of getting there? Where will you go next, once you have accomplished your dreams? If you can be happy, ecstatic even, doing your passion on a shoestring, in a small house on the wrong side of town, then you will learn to do it with grace with more money, more resources, better connections. And you will still be happy. Bonus! Might as well start loving what you do today.

Find five things you love about your passion you wouldn't change with unlimited resources, unlimited love, time or connections. These are things you do now.

1.
2.
3.
4.
5.

OK, OK. Now list five things that would be so much better if you could "make it" (start your own business, get a contract, publish a book, buy a house, go to college, etc.)

1.

2.

3.

4.

5.

If you don't feel like you have any passion, start looking for one. Ask your friends what they love. Try on their hobbies, sports, friends, interests, or careers. Go to a bookstore or library and browse the stacks. Grab any book that interests you. When you have ten titles or so, assess your collection. Is there a theme? Or several? Magic? Golf? Travel? Turtles? Are they all sleek and shiny or soft colors or is there color trend (maybe you are a designer)? Are people featured in all the titles (maybe counseling, research or autobiographies)? Perhaps you dream of visiting foreign lands, exploring historic times or visiting different cultures someday?

It doesn't matter what you love it loves you as well. Passion feeds your soul and you cannot afford to have it missing from your life. Your life may be busy with family, work, church or any number of obligations, but your passion can have space, too. For many, they think about it many times of the day anyway, even when they regret they are not doing it. You may as well enjoy it by participating in it.

It's your life! Start living it.

# In Sickness And In Health

Business as usual, that's what we like. That's what we crave when everything goes awry. It's easy to be patient and content when things are going our way. It's another story when we are hurting, frustrated or scared. These are times when we must find our faith.

If you are angry when you get sick, when life doesn't turn out like expected, or you feel it will never be done, look inside and find your faith. It may be there for only a moment, a fleeting gleam of hope that the sky will open up again to let sun through. That's all you need- one moment of faith. Then another.  Then another. Soon, the day will pass, then the month, and the year.

It may not take as long as you think. Perhaps you think you are at an ending, when you are truly beginning anew. It is a matter of breathing deeply, finding faith and stepping forward. Your destiny awaits you. Times of struggle are not the times we should give in, for they will not last. The victory on the other side will be the sweeter for having struggled through it.

Do not be afraid that it will last forever. Whatever it is, it will pass. Even our greatest seasons will eventually lull gently into warm moments of content. Life is cycles of growth, rest, stress and initiation. One moment we are struggling through the darkness of winter, only to behold one day that the crocus has pushed through the snow. We no longer need our winter clothes, our extra wood for the fireplace, our fortitude for long winter nights. Spring has arrived. We now must dig out our gardening tools, uncover our flowerbeds and prepare for summer's heat.

In relationships, we see the cycles profoundly. In a smaller cycle, we see a couple fall in love. Suddenly, life is bright and alive, filling with interest and exciting possibilities. We divest ourselves of solitary life, joining forces to stand against the world. Spring has come. Children come, careers grow, homes are bought and sold. We age. We grow together. Time passes and the trees turn colors. Fall is coming. We relax into the change of seasons, preparing for the upcoming darkness while enjoying the lovely autumn light while it remains. Eventually, the night sky becomes more dominant as winter blankets the world in quiet and restoration. We bury our loved ones in this quiet time, make new plans, take stock of our supplies, our desires, and our possible paths for the upcoming year. Meanwhile, grandchildren are born. New houses are built. Life continues.

In your own life, you may feel fallow, unrested, worn to the bone. This is temporary. Do not fear that seasons will not change again, for they must do so. Consider what season you are in. What comes next? Can you see how your current season is preparing you for the next? It is not wrong to consider that if you are in the heat of summer, to consider that you are about to approach a lovely autumn where you enjoy your harvest. Then you will take your winter season to rest, then replant in your spring. Or, if you are in winter and feeling like the sun will never return, have you considered what you will plant in spring, even though your fields are frozen solid at the moment (although they are not really, it only appears so)?

Think on your season. Which one are you in personally?

Career:
Money:
Love:
Health:
Spirit:

What season is your family in?

Can you see how you might grow from these seasons? Can you see how each is necessary to foster the next step in your life?


Perhaps everything feels wonderful. Are you thankful now? Do you see how your past led you to this wonderful place of abundance, character and fulfillment?

Name your worst winter:

Name your favorite fall, a time when you enjoyed the harvest of your labor:

Our darkest days seem un-heavenly, but there is faith available even in the times of greatest need. It may feel as though you walk alone, but you are never alone. Call it what you will, the Universe, God, Allah, The Divine -you are always in the company of the stuff that made you. There is a poem that says when you only see one set of footprints in the sand on your beach of life; it is a time when you are being carried. How else would you make it through those dark nights? Do not fear. You are not alone. You must only take stock of your season and see where you are in the cycle.

Some periods of our lives bring many changes. In our twenties, we see many friends married, babies born, companies formed, careers embarked upon. We see our grandparents and great grandparents pass. Our thirties see a time of relative calm, then we launch into our forties and fifties when see changes begin anew. Our children marry, have their own children, sometimes our parents witness this, sometimes they do not. Eventually, our generation moves to the front line. We witness our mortality in our friends, our allies, sometimes younger than us, as they pass into the beyond. We wonder if we have lived enough, strived enough, laughed enough, because next it may be our turn. This is a new season. We can choose to weather it with calm, peaceful in the knowledge that we are seeing a natural change. Or we can fight it and suffer.

This does not mean to go gently into old age, nor does it mean to give up. It means life is to be lived at all stages, in all forms of health and well being, and to leave no regrets. Illness and death can be a somber reminder to never take this life for granted. Take the trip. Make the phone call. Write the letter. Start the job. Move to the sun/rain/island. You have not a moment to spare. They will all add up eventually.

Do you have a nagging voice in your head that tells you to do something? What is it saying? Do you know that you have been putting off something very important to you?

Name it:

Why have you waited?
1.

2.
3.
4.
5.

That's a lot of reasons not to do it. Are there any that are really just excuses? Cross them out.

Now look at the remaining list. Which reason could you cross off this week? This month? This year?

This week:
This month:
This year:

Now, listen to fear that comes up. Write the first three things that come into your head:
1.
2.
3.

Are they real reasons? Write back to them, tell them why you can do it. Reverse the sentence.

Example: I can't start a business, now I am too old.

Change it into: I can start a business, and I have years of experience.

Why should you do it:
1.
2.
3.

What will happen if you don't do it:
1.

2.
3.

And finally, what will happen if you do it?:
1.
2.
3.
4.
5.

Make a decision. Life is but a moment, no matter what season you are in. Each moment becomes a chain in the time of our lives. Have no regrets. Leave no stone unturned. This is your life, and you owe it to yourself to be happy, fulfilled and leave this earth with no regrets. It is never too late to begin. In some cases, it may serve you to be older, wiser, and proven. Take a chance. All you have to lose is your fear.

# Who You Truly Are

Don't worry so much about pleasing other people. You are perfect just the way you are. We don't say that vey much these days, but the fact is, you are the only you in the world. Perhaps you don't look like anyone else, you act differently or you just can't relate to this world we live in. How refreshing; someone is daring to live life on their own terms.

You may be afraid of who you truly are. Maybe you are great and fear the thoughts that come into your head. You tell yourself you are meant for more. You hear a voice edging you on, saying that you can change things, invent things, or conquer a field. Or maybe you are secretly miserable and you are afraid to listen to that voice that tells you to rearrange your whole life, which means you will be changing everything, and right quick.

These are not the voices of desperation or delusion. This is the voice of reason. This is the voice of your soul, telling you to get it together. The tone of the voice is insistent, often tinged with urgency. It knows your darkest secrets, your talents and fears, your destiny waiting to be fulfilled. It won't let you get away with anything that doesn't suit you at your deepest level. It's the Jiminy Cricket of your mind, just waiting to send you on a quest for something great.

Don't wait. Now is the time to do that thing you have been waiting on. The fact that you hear a voice telling you to get it done means something- you have been putting it off far too long. You know it, too. Intuition works like this: first you get a feeling you should "do" something. You ignore it. The voice grows louder, denying the thought. The voice begins calling to you and you try to ignore it. Things begin to go wrong in your life, pointing you on the way towards something you need to do. You start hearing the thought when you are sleeping. Your mind is trying to tell you some truth you refuse to acknowledge. The longer you wait, the more persistent it becomes. Finally, you surrender. You recognize the peace, the quiet of mind and heart when you repeat the statement and acknowledge the truth. Your heart is speaking to you.

What have you been denying about yourself?

I really want to:
1.
2.
3.
4.
5.

If only I could:
1.
2.
3.
4.
5.

Sometimes our fears are so bad that we can't even say them out loud. We need to witness them, though, because on our insides they are wreaking havoc. Lay it out here, you don't have to say it to anyone but yourself.

My greatest fear is:

Is your fear that you are not enough? That you won't be loved? So is everyone else's. We all fear that we don't have what it takes or that people will reject us if we do what we really need to do. The very thing that we resist will launch us into a very different realm because we are making such a huge leap of faith. We are daring to put our very essence on the line. We risk our identities when we change, even if it is from a false self to a more authentic one. This is a big change.

Our loved ones don't always understand, that much is true. That's because they love us. Just the way we are, in fact. However, they may deepen their love for us when we make changes for the better. How will you know if you don't try? As we become a truer version of us, we will invariably make changes. The question is, are you willing to listen to your guidance and have faith that everything will be okay? Because that nagging voice is only going to grow in strength and intensity until you do something about it. You can drink, sleep, eat, exercise, or work it away, but it will never quit. Might as well deal with it earlier than later.

It doesn't really matter what you decide to do in this life. It's how you choose to feel. Some things will go badly, some better than expected, some just as planned. We are not in control. We try to pretend we are, but that is an illusion. We have all had days when a surprise changed everything we had planned. In a moment, we could lose everything, change our minds, fall completely apart or in love. It's not really up to us. We are at the mercy of the winds at times it seems. What we do have is a right to choose how we live this life.

It's not enough to be just satisfied. You have something special to offer, something special to do here. What is it? What are you great at? What would you want to be good at? It doesn't have to be grandiose. When you think about it, were great painters truly more than people fascinated with light and color? Don't musicians strive to create emotion with instruments? We are, at heart, very simple people. I am not denigrating any great deed or person, but illustrating that a very simple desire can produce great results. Sometimes we look at ourselves and feel inadequate to our desires. We think, "I am but a lowly....". So was Jesus. Think of yourself in terms of what you desire to create or change in the world, not so much about how you are going to accomplish it. Having a direction is important, but a drive that stems from a desire to serve will never lead you astray, no matter how many twists and turns the roads brings. How many times have you heard someone say that they humbly wanted to do X and ended up doing a magnificent Y? Often, that what makes news stories so intriguing, the result was unexpected success, yet somehow perfect.

Don't sell yourself short. Being a great parent might be the most important thing anyone has done. It's noble. Being a great neighbor, a kid's friend, a good sibling. All these things count as your path. Yes, you may feel led to create, invent, entrepreneur or explore, but your don't have to. Maybe you need to bravely retire, a little ahead of time, simply because you are ready. You don't need permission. Maybe you want a different line of work. Not a rock star, not a supermodel, not a celebrity, just something you have always wanted to try. Maybe you need to move to a different place. Maybe you always loved red but your mom told you it wasn't your color- wear it anyway! Get false lashes and highlights if you want. Paint your house purple, inside and out. Start asking yourself what your really want and then wait for an answer It will surely come.

Name three things you shouldn't do that you were told not to do (but you really want to do anyway):
1.
2.
3.

Name the person you most crave permission from:

Write yourself a note from them, giving you permission to be you as you are- just as you are. Read it aloud three times, and then dispose of it (a fireplace works nicely).

Name three things you think are delightfully quirky about yourself:
1.
2.
3.

If they were superpowers, how would you save the world with them?
1.
2.
3.

What superpower would you choose, if you could have any in the world?

Why?

Write one criticism people might say about your

superpower:

Now tell them why you can save their butts:

A superhero needs a costume. Pick one item, found, bought or created, that symbolizes your superpower that you can wear or keep near you: a feather or a cape of satin? A tiara? A wand? A badge? It can be silly or serious, as long as it means something special to you. Keep it safe. Honor it as an outward sign of an inward dream. It's your Superman "S".

You are perfect just the way you are. You are the only you we have. You are enough, and then some.

# It Only Takes One Day to Change Your Life...

400 years won't change anyone else's.

It's so easy to judge another's life. What we could be doing instead is changing our own. A simple decision can change so much in so little time. One moment can define our lives. One step can start a revolution in our minds.

Changing another person is not so easy. Nor is it advisable. You are really just pushing your will on another when you criticize, give advice or threaten someone else to change the way they think, act, look or behave. People need an opportunity to grow on their own. So many people these days are offended, annoyed or angered by other people, sometimes for trivial offenses. This is really an opportunity to cultivate our own patience, values, and frame of mind. It really doesn't matter how people act, it is up to us to react in a way in alignment with our spiritual growth.

If we only respond to angry drivers by becoming angry ourselves, we run the risk of becoming part of an endless chain of bad reactions to frustrating situations. When one person responds in anger, say, to their spouse in the morning, then is driving upset and offends you, who then arrives at work upset, who then criticizes a fellow staff member who then yells at their spouse when they get home...well, you see how it all runs downhill at that point.

Your response to situations is the only one you can control- no one else's. Responding in a manner of which in accordance with your values is not only keeping you calm, but it breaks the cycle of retribution and anger in our world. If you struggle with constantly angry about other people's behaviors, it is wise to ask yourself these two questions:

1) Do I surround myself with people who are my spiritual, intellectual or emotional peers?
2) Am I angry all the time?

If you are not around people who share your ideals, it can be very difficult to appreciate the differences in a real world scenario. For example, if you are an artist working in a bank, perhaps you can see why your peers don't "get you" if you consider that repetition, strict adherence to policy and ability to follow orders (something you abhor) is something they value to make a bank function well. It's obvious in that example, but consider if you and your best friend are matched in every way but one. You both love to walk, love animals, like the same restaurants, etc. But what if one of you really needs quiet to recharge yourself, yet the other needs the buzz of many, many unfamiliar people? See the problem? Do you curse out your friend? Of course not, you get together when you both want to do the shared activity.

Consider what other people are thinking when they behave the way they do. What's important to one person can be scarcely recognized by another. Let's face it; our upbringing bears tremendously how we expect people to act, as does our culture. One man's average behavior can be unforgivably rude to someone else. Some people find loud speaking out of character, others can't stand the soft spoken voice. A perfect example is shaking hands. Some people lament of soft grasps while others still complain of bone crushing clasps. Some women still prefer to turn up their hand, while others refrain from shaking. Chances are, you have a firm opinion regarding this, which is perfect. So does someone else. We have to learn to live and let live in the world.

Many times, we seek to delve into the minds of the people closest to us. We see their potential; their bright spirits and we press them to be the best we think they can be. We do this by lovingly criticizing them. Yes, we tell them to be different. We are doing this to please ourselves, not them. In fact, they are often not happy when we try to rearrange them in any way. We might mean well, but in the end, we are pushing ourselves away from love.

It takes courage to put aside our own fears regarding other people's behaviors. We do not have to like their behaviors to honor them as human beings. It is best to learn from their behavior and examine our reaction to it. When someone is unkind or rude, it does not give us license to be rude back. What would it accomplish? If they are truly uncaring, it won't matter what we do. Perhaps they have a different set of manners. The question is what do you really value? Why are you so offended if someone doesn't signal? Or they cut past a long line of traffic on an onramp? Does it really matter? What would happen if you went and shouted at a truly dangerous person wielding a gun? Would you feel as brave as you do giving someone the finger behind your wheel in the relative safety of your car? With today's technology, it's easy to be cruel behind a keyboard. Anonymously.

The truth is, we can stand up for who we are by becoming the qualities we want other people to have. Be the polite person at the grocer, the dry cleaner, and the deli. Take time to consider your responses. So many people are in such a hurry these days. Consider that many do not even stop long enough to realize they have forgotten to say "hello" or "thank you" or "how are you"? You can be a better person, for the world and yourself, if you choose to not let it bother you. If it is truly an injustice, take the necessary steps to bring about consciousness.

Think about what you value in people. List five traits:
1.
2.
3.
4.
5.

Do you see these traits in yourself?  Mark a Y for yes and an N for no next to each trait.

For the ones you think you embody, list three times in the last week when you have not been these things.
1.
2.
3.

So, you are not perfect. No big deal. No one is.

Think of one person you'd really like to change or give advice to:

List five things they need to know:
1.
2.
3.
4.
5.

Now, explain why you think they need your advice.

Now, write yourself a letter with these five things. They are things you need to know as well. That's why you can see areas in need of improving in your own life. Explain why you need to here this advice, right here, right now:

Next, list five things someone you love has told you to change about yourself that they are **dead wrong** about.
1.
2.
3.
4.
5.

Next, explain to them why you are perfect, just the way you are:

You are, in fact, perfect. So is everyone else. We often try to correct in other what we see as our own failings or weaknesses. Sometimes we also see a better vision of the world we want to create. Become a citizen of that world. Inspire someone with your kindness, grace, vision, peace and beauty. Let your light shine through. It could very well change someone's world in just a moment of time.

Notes:

# Debt, Guilt and Dumpster Diving in Your Soul

We all have issues in our lives that we are not proud of. We caused some of those ourselves; some were the results of other's actions. For some, these issues rule our lives. We let our sadness, guilt, and debt run our lives. These issues can cause feelings of unworthiness. This is not at all necessary.

There's no reason to ruin your self-esteem because you made mistakes, even if you made lots of them. Of course, you should try to make good choices, but consider that you are making mistakes because you are searching for something. Or you are learning something. It does not mean that you must stay in that place of discomfort.

Take out the trash! Doubtless you harbor regrets, everyone does, but what good does it do you to relive old wounds? Worse yet, you may try to hold onto the scars far longer than you were meant to. Lessons are learned from difficult times. We are then to release them and begin anew.

Our lives need not be guided by the decay of leaves fallen years ago. This world is to be cherished whole, full of life and prospering. When we hold onto old wounds, we fester the seed of discontent by living in the past. Reach out, soar, and shake off the mantle of regret holding you from walking lightly in this land.

You are already whole. You know what to do. So name it.

List three things you wish you had never done:
1.
2.
3.

Can you undo any of them? Mark a Y for yes or an N for no next to each item. If the answer is Y, undo it, make the call, write the letter, or pay the bill. If the answer is N, can you apologize? If you can, do so, as soon as possible.

If you cannot apologize or make amends, list three things that could make the biggest regret livable.
1.
2.
3.

Do one of them right now. Even just a tiny step forward will help. This is the garbage we live with in ourselves. We do not need it, we shouldn't want it, nor do we really need to go through it again. If you know it's garbage, toss it! (Nope, no recycling here. No one else needs it, either. Imagine a magic, totally green incinerator if you must.)

What do you feel guilty about?
1.
2.
3.
4.
5.

That's a lot to feel bad about. Make amends, if you can.

If you cannot, ask yourself if the guilt is serving another purpose. Is it your excuse to put off something? Are you afraid you will be rejected or unloved if you stop feeling guilty about it? What's your number one guilt?

How long should you feel guilty about this situation? Months? Years? Forever?

How long have you felt guilty about this? Months? Years? Since you can remember?

What purpose does it serve to feel bad about this situation? Do you think you learned your lesson? Would you ever repeat the steps that got you into your predicament? If the answer is no, write a letter to whomever you harmed.

List the reasons you feel terrible, really terrible about what happened:
1.
2.
3.

Pour out your heart. Truly tell the person, this could include yourself, why you wish it had never happened, never will happen again and what it has meant to you all this time. Ask for forgiveness. You really need it. Sign the letter. Hold the envelope to your chest and know that you have been forgiven. You have suffered enough. No one deserves a life sentence of guilt. Burn it, mail it, or toss it in the ocean. You are free.

The next time you want to feel rotten about the situation, remember that you have been forgiven. Think of this as a rotten old chair in your corner. You once had a party and it caught on fire. It's charred and stinking from when you threw a drink on it to put out the flames. Still, you keep it because it was once your grandmother's. It doesn't match your decor. It smells. You throw a sheet over it when company comes because it's a hideous eyesore. One day, you decide it's time. You take it to the curb. You breathe a sigh of relief that it's gone. Finally, you are free.

Until the garbage truck comes, maybe tomorrow, maybe the day after that, you will be tempted to bring back into your house. Don't even think about it. The hardest part was the decision to let it go. Now you must decide what to put in its place. Another old, stinky chair to haunt you for days to come, or a lovely new one that you love to sit in that guests choose foremost when they arrive?

Don't bury yourself in debt once you get out. Don't charge the card again, congratulating yourself on paying it off. It's different this time. You are different. Don't bring in that stinky old chair just because you need a place to sit one afternoon. Find something else to do with that space. Replace your guilt with praise. Say to your self, "Thank goodness that situation is all over with. I have felt bad long enough." Resolve to never feel bad again about that old chair. You never really used it to sit on anyway.

Don't let the crummy relationship come back, either. You know he/she/they are dirty old chairs. If you really want white leather or creamy yellow chenille, don't let anyone talk you into that old chair. Sure, it was once yours, but now it's on the curb. Walk away from it and don't even look out the window to see if it is still there. (That means, don't go stalking their Facebook page, just to "see".) If nothing else, imagine the look on your neighbors faces when you drag the trash into your house, not the other way around.

Feeling guilty because you have too much? That's survivor's guilt. Perhaps you have moved far beyond your humble origins. Your family and old friends accuse you of being "too good" for them because you decided to go to school, move out of the neighborhood, or get a better job. Are you doing everything you can to pass those blessings on? Are you paving a trail for other people, giving time or money to causes that can increase others? Are you nice to as many people as you can be? You have become a blessing to others. Take pride in your achievements. You can be gracious and humble while still holding the cars. How about being thrilled you can put your family to work or pay off their houses? Greater still, what if you can reach out beyond your community, to the state level, or even the national?

Wouldn't it be a blast to help someone across the world, someone you have never met? Count your blessings and give some away. You can prosper others by simply being kind. What good does success do if you feel guilty that you bought a lovely new chair after letting go of the old one? Does the chair really care? No, you do. You are afraid you will not be loved.

List three famous givers (of time, money, ideas) that you admire:
1.
2.
3.

Moneyed or not, they were generous with what they had. Be generous, feel not guilty that you have enough to share with others. If others seek to make you feel guilty, simply understand that they are struggling and that their actions are expected, if not desired. It is up to you to surge forth, continuing to prosper and share from your generous spirit.

There is no other way. Your guilt will not prosper anyone. Your fine heart will.

Notes:

# Who Do You Really Owe?

Bless yourself by saying thanks to those who have helped you upon your way. It is easy in this busy world to blame other people for things gone wrong on our lives, but what about the people who have made our lives so right? When was the last time you wrote a thank you note or an email for something that seems simple like raising you, feeding you, teaching you, making you laugh?

Often, we are so caught up being busy or harboring resentment that we forget to express our thanks on real and tangible ways. Consider writing your parents a letter, thanking them for all that they did right. Pass over the temptation to mention what you feel they did wrong, this is unimportant at the moment. You are making a list of things you like about yourself, really. How long is that list?

List five things you like about yourself:
1.
2.
3.
4.
5.

Next to the items above, write the name of the person you got that trait from. You can list yourself, if you need to, but really this is about acknowledging gifts others gave to you.

Do you spend time with these people? Are you calling them often enough? Do they know how much you owe them? They enriched your life, made you who you are. Tell them soon, before you miss the chance. Did you have a great teacher who turned you onto what is now a career you love? Did a neighbor or babysitter take care of you every day after school when your parent(s) had to work to put food on your table? What about a stranger who touched your life?

Think of your spiritual debt. Who haven't you paid yet? Who hasn't heard your voice tell them "thank you" or "I'm sorry"?

Name one person you really, really need to get a hold of:

Why do you avoid contacting them? Are you nervous, scared of what they might think? This gets harder as time goes on. Have you let years pass? It doesn't matter, you can always say what you need to say. It's never too late to make it right.

Name five times you apologized and it didn't seem to matter:

1.
2.
3.
4.
5.

How did it affect you? Did you feel resentment? Did you forgive, but not forget? Did you cross them off your list of friends? If it still bothers you, you need to say something. If the person is dead or gone, you can always write a letter

Read it out loud. Sign and seal it. You can then mail it, burn it or toss it out to sea. Just don't keep it! You need closure. So do they.

Do you spend time with people who love you? Cherish you? Comfort you? Or do you spend time with people who undervalue you, exploit you or simply tolerate you? Do you attend lots of functions you do not want to attend, just to get ahead at work? Meanwhile, does your family ask why they never see you? Do you frequently say you should call your mother/father/friend/sibling but never do it?

What's stopping you?
1.
2.
3.
4.
5.

If your number one answer is time- you are in luck! You can make more time in your life by deciding to do so.

List five things that you waste time on each week (yes, the Internet counts):
1.
2.
3.
4.
5.

Next to the items above, list approximately how much time you waste on each activity each week. Is it a workday, another night's sleep, or an entire additional job? Decide if you want to limit one activity in its entirety or a little from each.

Do you enjoy your time wasters? If not, look at those first. Perhaps it's your commute. Can you somehow combine your commute with something more quality? For instance, could you ride public transportation and text friends you are out of contact with, or call them? If you never get to read anymore, your commute is the perfect time. Then, you have more time with your family or friends when you are at not work.

Do you surf the Internet endlessly? Decide to cut a quarter to half of your time this next week by setting a timer. Or do double duty on your lunch hour, not at home when your child wants to read a book. What about making web surfing a family experience? You could all surf together, learning and discussing. Afterwards, you could have a small quiz and the winner gets a prize- voila, instant game show.

If your time wasters are daily chores, consider ways to make them fun. Most times, we multitask anyway. Why not make two things fun together or involve someone else? Try washing dishes while reviewing your mental lists or your voice practice. Do knee bends at the sink to get in some much needed exercise. Analyze your green footprint by measuring your water consumption and composition of your dish soap.

Your time wasters may be combined with unwinding, like watching TV or recreational drinking. Look at your list and consider how important these activities really are in relationship to your other needs.

Name three areas of your life that need attention (health, family, love, friends, creative, spiritual, work, organization):
1.
2.
3.

Does one of your time wasters directly affect these areas? Rank them in order of importance. Now rank your time wasters. Line up your number one time waster to the area in need of the most attention. Which one is most important?

Which are you willing to give up?

This could be a very startling realization for you. If number one is drinking versus spouse, you may have a crisis on your hands. Chances are, if it feels this dire; there is something else at work.

Do you give yourself enough time? Are you stressed? Many times these days, people don't include themselves worthy of attention. They feel selfish for wanting time alone, time to think, or to relax. They want to be there for their families, their friends, their coworkers and children.

List three things you should or badly want to do for yourself (but don't):
1.
2.
3.

After each item write the reason why you don't do it (for example, feel guilty, not enough time or don't know how to) next to it. Circle the one you need the most. How long will it take? Chances are it's easier to carve out a little time for it each day by eliminating a time waster.

Name the time waster you are cutting so you can have the thing you need so badly:

You just won a major hurdle.

Notes:

# Find Five Regrets

What often holds us back can bring us far more forward when we let it go. Chances are, there are unresolved issues in your life that leave you sleepless at night. Clearing up these issues can quickly recover a sense of lost ground or balance.

Life is not a game. Winning or losing is irrelevant to whether or not you will be happy. In the end, we must all deal with our leaving this place. When your life winds down to ashes, what will you regret? Big or small, these are the stakes that matter. Ask yourself, have you lived your life to the fullest? Have you spent all your talents on the pursuit of your dreams? Did you make yourself and others happy? There is nothing wrong with fame, fortune, notoriety or achievement, but if what you really want is a family, you are not truly succeeding.

We all have things in our lives that we wish we had done differently, but letting them weigh you down will steal your zest for living. Sometimes we regret not going for it when we really wanted to. Maybe you wanted to study abroad or major in a different subject in college. Maybe you lost touch with the person you feel like was a soul mate. Don't let that stop you from doing it now.

You can change it all! Sometimes we can change the event, right some wrongs, undo some damage or make a second chance for ourselves. Other times, we must change the way we view the event. We must learn to forgive and forget, admit we were wrong or just plain let it go.

List five regrets:
1.
2.
3.
4.
5.

Which one keeps you up at night? Circle that one. Next, choose the one you could make fast progress on today.

List three steps to crossing off the most easily fixed regret:
1.
2.
3.

Do one right now. Yes, really, right this moment.

How did it feel to take a step forward? Emotional? Brilliant? Are you filled with a sense of relief? This is the pressure building up on your insides, day in and day out. It takes a portion of your mind, your concentration, your attention and your body to deal with this little corner of your mind all the time. And this is the little regret!

Let's look at our numbers 2, 3, and 4 on the list. Can any be solved with a little effort? Think about whether it can be fixed (F), viewed differently (V) or if it needs to be let go of (L). Mark each item with the appropriate letter.

For (F) fixed write down three steps to make peace with it:

1.
2.
3.

For the (V) viewed differently items, write out these statements:

If I wanted to, I could see this as an opportunity to:

Someone else might see this as:

If I weren't so _____, I could see this as _____.

For the items marked (L) let go of, write out these three statements:

Now I see that:

I can let go now because:

I am thankful this occurred because I learned:

Do you see how you can make up a lot of ground in simply viewing your regrets as something different? How about how you can change some into goals? If your life seems lackluster and your regrets coincide with your dreams not coming true, this is a great opportunity to look at why you aren't going for them.

Which one of your regrets would you be most afraid of dying with? Which one would disturb you even in death? Picture yourself at your funeral. Did you finish what you set out to do? If not, look to your regret list. Which one needs to fixed and can become a goal?

Say it here:

List three reasons it won't happen:
1.
2.
3.

List three reasons it might happen:
1.
2.
3.

List three reasons it will happen:
1.
2.
3.

The first list is your excuses- cross them all off. They no longer count. The second list is your hopes. You think it could happen- maybe, just maybe. Are any of them related to your excuse list? For example, (the excuse) "It won't happen because I am too old", is related to your hopeful statement: It could happen because there was just someone older than me in the news doing it. These sections are part of your faith and your doubt going around in circles chasing each other.

The list of reasons you know it will happen is now a to do list. You are confident that it can be done and the list is how you are going to get there. Many times our excuses are really just fear dressed up in rationality. Sometimes we are more afraid of failing than we are of not trying, but we must invert those two so that we are afraid to regret more than to fail. Failing at least means we tried, and for many of us, that means a far more peaceful conscience than never attempting something.

Hopefully, your regrets can launch you into a less worried state of mind. Living in the past makes it harder to go forward. Big regrets can weigh a person down into depression and a loss of faith. Be brave with your regrets, you have nothing to lose in bringing them to light and letting them go.

# Put Your House In Order

It's time to clean up. What needs to go? What needs a better home? What could you really do without? Let's take inventory of what in your life needs to get swept away. Be brave. You can do this.

Let's look at your physical home. Is it tidy? Are there dead plants everywhere? Does a layer of dust coat everything? Is it a cheerful mess? Is it overly clean, devoid of all mementos and personal touch?

Your home is your sanctuary. It is also a reflection of your current state of mind. Full of junk, it can clog your mind with unfinished business, half hearted work, and neglected duties. A home full of love can still be messy, but order prevails. If your house is without love, it will fill with debris, unwanted items and cobwebs. You deserve the best, so get ready to let go of the clutter. Prepare a place to rest, to nourish yourself and to create a safe place to open up to possibilities. Create a peaceful atmosphere. Move some furniture. Paint a wall or two.

Which part of your home suffers the most? Do you keep your papers and work near where you rest? Does each member of your household have their own space, a place where they can be themselves? It doesn't matter if you have a small home. What matters is how you share the space. Does your home feel discordant, loud and have lots of activity? Do you wish it was otherwise?

Is your home lonely? Is it dark and stuffy? Could you use some light? What about some paint or a plant? If you live alone and feel like it's pointless to decorate, think about what kind of home you would like to share with another person.

Everybody has their own needs regarding what they need from a home. Some need quiet, some like rich decor, some prefer simple and restful colors. No one, however, needs to live in disarray or chaos. If you have children, it is not the same kind of chaos. While children can delight with laughter, squeals and play, true chaos has no joy. It robs one of the ability to relax, predict, rest or plan. The garage that serves as a dumping ground is an example. A haphazard pile of mail that goes unanswered for weeks on end is another. A closet full of "someday" clothes is yet another.

What needs to go?

Be honest. You know what it is.
1.
2.
3.

What displeases you in your home?
1.
2.
3.

What disgusts you in your home?
1.
2.
3.

What makes your home perfect?

1.

2.

3.

It's not really about your house. If you live with people, you probably answered those people as what makes your home perfect. Maybe it's your pets or the feeling you get when you make a special dinner for one and serve it on the good plates. The feeling you have is peace, joy and rest. This is the place you get comfortable. This is where your mind can relax and let loose from the confines of judgment in the outside world. The place is your spiritual home, not necessarily your physical one.

Let's look at this from another angle. If you can't be happy in your place, how can you be happy anywhere? This is the place where you set the rules. People come and go because you let them. Generally, people who live together have agreed upon the rules that govern the domicile. Even college roommates seem to work out a system for handling diverse schedules, needs and desires, why not you?

What makes you crazy in your home? Guess what? It's the same thing that makes you crazy out in the world. It doesn't matter who started it, but coworkers who leave dishes in the sink makes you as crazy as your teenager doing it at home. Do you feel unheard by your spouse, but also by your boss? What about worrying about home when you are work, but worrying about work when you are at home? It's all part of the same thing.

This is our mental home. This is really where we live, day in, day out.

This is the space we inhabit spiritually as well. Sit with that for a moment. You may go home, turn away from the outer world and find deep and satisfying peace every time you come home. Chances are, however, that you trade work chaos for home chaos of some kind. Whether you have no time to clean properly, your family misses you and demands your time when what your really want is a book and a glass of wine, or you are pursuing another job or interest at home, you are not truly letting go at the end of the day.

Day after day, these stresses pile up until one day, there's a garage sale waiting to happen in our lives. Not one more thing can fit into the closet. The towels have holes, every last one of them. The kids grew two inches overnight, one's even got a new piercing. Life has been sneaking up on us. We may put out fires, one after another, but all that leaves is holes in our carpet.

When was the last time you had time to rearrange your furniture, your home, or your life? Has it been it months, years or never?

Your furniture:
Your home:
Your life:

No, there's nothing wrong with keeping the chair in the corner for twenty years (assuming you dust under it). Realize that reflects your state of mind. There's also nothing wrong with not re-arranging your life or your home, assuming it all is in the order you need it to be. Note that need and want are not always the same. One example is if you want it to be a home for entertaining because you have life that requires that, yet you desperately need a space to unwind where you can leave out your art supplies, model cars, karaoke equipment, etc. Make sure your home is a place where you can be you, period. If not, a revamp might be in order.

Do you have an activity that you need to be alone to do, even in a home full of people? Maybe you are shy, scared or embarrassed to have a witness when you do it. Or maybe it just requires a quiet space. That's OK. Things of this nature could be practicing an instrument or sport, learning to paint or dance, building complex models, doing yoga, etc. Do you have a space to do something like this?

What's something you really want to do at home alone but can't find a space to do?

What would happen if you do it in front of people?
1.
2.
3.

There may be a part of you that you feel you need to hide, for better or worse. Consider if it's something that is a solitary activity that requires introspection and concentration or if it's really a matter of fearing what people will think of you. It's a shadow side of your world. Consider taking it a little more public in a way that feels safe.

Could go to a park where you would still have quiet? Could you invite someone who does your activity as well to be with you, perhaps in a silent session in your home? The key is to feel safe when you are venturing out.

List three ways you could take your activity public and still feel very safe doing it, if you had to:
1.

2.
3.

The reason to take it public is to own it. It's part of you, perfect, beautiful you. You don't have to hide. You can be strong in your peace outside of your home. This part of you needs to see daylight, and it's high time you acknowledge that you need it. Once you can have peace in your mind, you can have peace in any house in the world, especially your own.

# 5 Minutes A Day Is Your 10%

How do you give? What's your tithe?

Sometimes we feel like we have nothing left to share, but the truth is our greatest gift can be our time. Our deepest joy resides in helping others, especially when they are close to us.

Think about a time when someone helped you for no good reason. They didn't have to. They just did it. When was the last time you did something for someone and expected no reward? Maybe it has been a long time, especially if you are feeling under a lot of pressure in your life.

Have you thought about what five minutes a day spent giving could bring to your life? Imagine what a note, a letter, or even a text could do to brighten someone's day? Imagine being a checker at the grocery store around dinnertime and you are the one person who truly smiles, says thanks, and turns that person's day around? Would you do it?

Some will say that giving is really something you do for yourself, and that is true to the extent that you receive as well as when you give. It is very hard to give, truly give, with selfish motives. Even if you expect something in return (which is unadvised), you are adding to the positive in the world. Life changing giving comes from the heart, though, and should be thought out at the purest level.

Start thinking in terms of what other people need. Start with your closest circle. Does your brother need a friend to talk to or pal to go pick out curtains with? Does your elderly aunt need someone to have lunch with? Does your next-door neighbor need help because they can't get on a ladder or mow their lawn? Start where you are.

Name three people who need something that costs little or nothing:
1.
2.
3.

Can you give something you have; time, some money or some knowledge? What about your company? Can you fix some food or beverages and spend half an hour saying hello to someone you know is going through a divorce or a death?

The world needs you. Just you. Not even your money or your resources. You are enough to change a broken heart, lift someone up and turn it around. Kindness can move mountains. You may not believe it yet, but start practicing and it may astonish you how many people are shocked by a willing heart and a kind hand.

We may live in a world full of stressed people who worry over many things, but you can become a shining light of love and hope for them. (Never mind that your own life will also benefit form a blessed mindset.) It isn't even that difficult.

Everyday, you can give of yourself. You may think you already give too much, that you are exhausted and worn out. This is a different type of giving. This is a portion of your joy, your spirit. You always have more of that. In fact, giving from your deepest self replenishes your ability to give more, thrive and be a blessing to others.

If you find giving wears you out, think about what you are focusing on when you give. Are you giving something you cannot afford to let go of, like money you really need, your happiness as you listen to a friend endlessly complain, or an item you feel guilty about having that you give away because you feel you don't deserve it. That's sacrificing, not necessarily giving. Maybe you can live without something, but if it makes you feel awful to give it, it may not be the right way to give.

What the world needs is love. You have more than you know to give. To walk in love, you only need to focus on the joy of being alive. Like a new dawn, your joy will spill over onto others. They, in turn, will spill joy onto more people. Your walking in love will create a ripple on the ocean.

It does not have to be loud. You can walk quietly in love, be peaceful and radiate good to others without even opening your mouth. Try practicing smiling at strangers each day. If nothing else, watch their reaction. Many will be shocked. Once upon a time, it was common practice to greet people on the street. Why not bring that practice back? Maybe it's time to introduce yourself to the neighbor you have lived next to for five years.

Let the world see how beautiful you are! Your family loves you. They know you best, and they think the world of you. Trust them, they are right. Yes, that includes families of coworkers, colleagues and the families we make. Your closest people are your family. Believe them. They see you and want to share you with the world. They are your greatest fans.

List five things you are good at (cooking, repairs, mechanics, playing video games, etc.):

1.

2.

3.

4.

5.

Have you ever considered that maybe your gift can bridge two generations? Have you ever tried to get your Grandma on Facebook? Or taught your neighbor who loves chess about the online version? You may think your gift is small, but the world is made up of details. Great trees only exist because leaves give them nutrients. Don't sell your gifts short! Your love of sewing may make you an outsider in high school, but have you tried the senior center? You might just find a few new ladies who fight over your company!

If all else fails, smile. That's right. Just smile at everyone you meet. The power of a smile can win over most unhappy people. You will feel better if you smile. Don't fake it, don't be crass. Genuinely try to laugh at difficult situations. They too, will pass. Everything goes more smoothly if you give it a little smile.

Make everyday giving part of your 10%. Of course, giving money to support causes is wonderful. Giving your time is even better. Giving your energy is the best you can give. How would you life change if you could take inward pride in really turning a situation around for a person? What if the first time they felt valued came from you? Do you know that many people feel unworthy of love or value? Can you imagine never feeling appreciated or so lonely that you only talk to your pet each day?

Is that you?

Think about what it would mean to you if your neighbor showed up with your favorite dessert and a half hour to spend on a rainy day? Sure, it might be awkward at first, but remember your first dates? It's kind of fun to be excited and nervous. Think about how expectant you were to have some great fun on that date! You also know that they care enough about you to initiate contact.

Take some time in your life to connect with people in need. It may feel like there is lack everywhere once you start looking for it, but you will know when the time is right to step in. You never know, you could change a life forever, maybe even your own. If you are lonely and feeling disconnected, reach out to help someone else. You can feel strong in your ability to reach inside and give, even when it feels like your well has run dry.

Start dreaming up ways to touch people. Make some anonymous gifts. Send flowers without a name. Pull your neighbor's trashcans in. Fold laundry you didn't put in the dryer. Donate to causes. See if you can find out how to volunteer for your favorite charities. Start being nicer, even if you had a rough day.

Be brave. You can get involved in other people's lives and have it cost you little. This is relationship, through and through. You are giving and getting at the same time. Your relationship with yourself is improving as you cast a wider net of influence. Don't be afraid to share of your greatest gift-your self and your time.

All it takes is a few minutes a day to change a life.

# Smile and the World
# Smiles With You

It's so easy to give a smile. We think it is easier to pay an eye for an eye, but unhappiness breeds only more unhappiness. You will never truly feel better giving another your spite or anger instead of your love. You may feel that they have mistreated you and that you deserve to treat them poorly, but it will only lower your energy level. In your heart, you will know it's not the right way to happiness. Even if you momentarily feel vindicated by cursing someone out, yelling or insulting someone, the effects are truly short lived.

The world you inhabit is ultimately determined by how you view it. As you begin to live in love, the world will appear in love as well. If you chose to live in anger, fear or even resignation, your outer world will reflect these traits. It is not how the world is, but how you see the world. Think of a recent day that did not go well. What were you thinking about? When you were late, did you get in a bad mood, curse out drivers or become tight and stressed? What would happen if you chose to simply not let it bother you?

It seems so simple, and it is, but it can be difficult to accomplish at first. We are not practiced in radiating our love each day. Sometimes we will radiate for our partner, our pets or our children, but what of ourselves? Each and every one of us needs love. We do not "get" love; we become it. Love is an action, an attitude, and a mindset. You certainly do not have to love traffic, but you can love your commute all the same. You have a job, there is a sky above you, scenery to look at, people to greet if you use mass transit. If you are only satisfied when each day is perfect and goes your way, you will be deeply dissatisfied with life.

What are you bringing to your encounters? Are you bringing an open mind, a willingness to make each interaction pleasant and rewarding? Or are you concentrating on your needs, your frustrations, or your pain? If you are suffering, you may very well feel like you must "get" something from others. However, everything you need is already inside of you. You simply must remember how to walk in love.

Start with yourself. Think of something that makes you smile, no matter where you are. Let that feeling radiate from your heart. At some point, you may break out into a grin. Next time you are in traffic, think of this thing. It is very difficult to be grateful, walking in love, and be mad at the same time. Love is more powerful. Love can transmute anything into a neutral energy.

You are not doing this for others, although they will benefit. You are doing this to heal yourself. You need love. If you tend only to think of it as a romantic notion, think about how you feel when a loved one is close. Most likely, you want to give to them. It is unlikely that you are thinking about what you need to get from them. If you are, you need to turn up what you are giving, so you can receive more. It's an infectious attitude, but you are not trying to change the other person at all. You are transforming yourself.

Smiling is an easy way to radiate love. It's a natural

extension of the emotional state of love. Certainly, you might think that you will be judged as you drive in traffic or walk down the street smiling. Perhaps, perhaps not. It is very possible that you may make a new friend, but you will definitely enjoy the journey more than if you are stressed, irritated and unhappy. Emotions are contagious- every one of them. Whatever attitude you are bringing to the situation is going to quickly be shared.

Likewise, it is important to shield yourself from unhappy attitudes. There is no way to avoid certain unhappy individuals, so you must decide in advance that you will have a good attitude, even if you think it is going to be a difficult encounter. Consider if you head into the DMV in a hurry, annoyed that someone grabbed your parking spot, and you face a long line. You can endure (suffer), aggravate the situation (foot tapping and grumble) or choose love. In love, you get this moment to rest. You have nothing to do, nowhere to go, no one to be. You are here for this moment, nothing else. When was the last time you let your mind drop away as you took a pleasant moment to reflect in the middle of your hectic day? You now have a precious gift, time. You can meditate, text a friend or make a new one in the line. You could bring a book and catch up on some reading you missed. This, like all other encounters in life, is an opportunity to be happy, no matter what.

There really is no moment other than this one. This thought, this feeling, this embodiment of space is all there is. It will be then stored in our minds as memories. The past feels real, but it is also an illusion. The future is unknown. Of course, we all remember our pasts and plan for our futures. What is real, though, is the moment we are in. We cannot take it back when it is gone. Likewise, we cannot truly know how it will go. We can only live in the right now. When we choose love, we have fewer regrets because we are present, we speak with our hearts, and we make choices from a place of happiness.

Living out of love can be done, of course. You can go through life feeling disconnected, angry, fearful, alienated or self righteous, but if you are only happy when you are right, other people are perfect, or everyone understands you, your moments of happiness will be few and far between.

Think about your most unhappy days, ones that occur with some frequency (not a catastrophic event like a death or divorce). Do you have a person who becomes your nemesis on those days? This could be a coworker, your spouse, your boss or someone you encounter regularly like a tollbooth person or a checker. Perhaps you just hate the grocery shopping or errands you must run.

List three tasks you cringe and loath even thinking about:
1.
2.
3.

Is there someone else involved? List the person by each activity number above:
1.
2.
3.

If you could change this person, what would you change about them in this situation?
1.
2.
3.

Realize you have to be that thing you want to change in the other person. First of all, you wouldn't recognize the need if you couldn't see it in yourself. Second, you can't change anyone else. All you are left to change in this situation is yourself. You get to receive by giving more of the thing that is needed. Bring that healing emotion, trait, or attitude to the encounter. The truth is, you are adding to the problem by anticipating a problem in the first place. Then you want to make the situation different by changing another. Change tactics! Bring a smile. Disarm a surly banker with your charm, your friendly attitude and your willingness to give a good customer experience.

There's no reason to be fake or dishonest. In fact, this is very important. You truly must find something good to think on when you are in the moment. One thing! You only need to find one thing. If you can't think about something that makes you want to smile wherever you are.

Never mind if the person you think is your nemesis doesn't catch on right away. If you have been interacting in a negative manner for some time, it might throw them off guard when there is a sudden change. If you are shy or feel insecure, it might feel odd to pursue a bright attitude when it isn't being returned. Ignore the impulse to pull back. You are doing for yourself first and foremost. This is your moment. Are you going to love it or let it get you down?

Each moment is your moment for greatness. You might face adversity in your day, but your attitude will make all the difference once you are through it. Set a goal for tomorrow to live in love. There's no need to tell anyone you are doing it. See if anything goes more smoothly. Maybe you will notice something you have never seen on the way to work before. Perhaps you will resolve a conflict with an unhelpful coworker. Maybe your children or spouse will respond differently when you walk forward in love through the door at the end of the day. Chances are, at least you will find most of the day goes more smoothly. Whenever you feel like you are getting frustrated or down, rely on your favorite things to pull you through. Take a moment to relax, let everything go and breathe in the moment. Take note of the people who respond to your open heart. You may be surprised to find out who they are.

You may even find out the person who needed your love the most was you.

# Fear Not, Said the Angel...

Fear not the things of your life. You are really very safe. Your person, your body, your life and possessions, they are all safe. Fear will rob you of more peace of mind than any thief. Fleeing a situation because of the trappings of your mind will steal your peace, your love and your growth. Fear is not needed in your life any longer.

You may have lived through much. Let it go. You are not alone. You are not to worry. Everything is fine, will always be fine, is forever fine. You are here to love, the absence of fear. Fear means to not accept something, the opposite of love. Love means to welcome it in, whatever it may be.

Fear shows up in many ways. Many times we do not see it for what it is. We call it responsibility, sensibility, or being safe. It evades definition because we can see the point. It makes sense to be fearful when it is wrapped up in common sense or tradition.

Fear cannot make you happy. It is an enemy of happiness, because where there is fear there is tension. Happiness thrives in acceptance and love. Fear creates an atmosphere where it is difficult to relax. Fear can drive us to many things that are not good for us, weaken our spirits and take us from the present moment. Fear often lives in the future, even if it is rooted in the past.

Your fear may feel very different from your neighbor's. What worries you may not even bother someone else. Likewise, you may not understand what all their fuss is about, either. Emotional, physical and psychological security comes with all kinds of risks, we think. The truth is, security only ever comes from one place, from within.

All worry is a form of fear. It may be feel like a good idea to worry over practical cares like your children at school or your health or your finances. Worry is not the same as action. It may feel as though we are doing something to prevent an ill result, but all we are doing is activating our adrenal system. Fretting over finances is not the same as making a plan, having discipline and seeing results because you followed through.

Consider useful fear, the type that makes you run from a burning building or react in traffic. That kind of fear is momentary, lasting only a few seconds. Worry, however, can last days, months, or even years before it responds to a real threat, if it ever does. Fear can serve you in good ways, but often times not the way we use it today. To worry that your children will not be safe on the ride to school is not the same as checking the bus driver records or assuring that they are well prepared to protect themselves from threats on their way. One action creates an opportunity to respond, while worry simply anticipates a perceived possible outcome of the situation. But, what if we worry about the wrong thing? For example, you teach your children to fear all strangers, but what if it is a friend who harms them? Or what if a random act of violence or nature comes from out of nowhere? Worry will imagine all kinds of scenarios going wrong, but since we truly never know what will happen, we can spend all our energy preparing for the wrong things. Useful fear addresses a threat in the moment. Not before, not after.

What do you worry about? Can you truly foresee a threat to you or your loved ones? Or are you reliving a past experience that you are projecting into the future? A great example is flying in an airplane. Turbulence is rarely life threatening, but once you have had a big drop or two, you will often remember that experience and every time the plane hits a small pocket of air, you will anticipate something larger. If you let the fear take over, you can ruin a perfectly safe flight worrying over every small current the plane encounters when there is never any real danger. Meanwhile, you failed to listen to the safety briefing or locate your nearest exit. In a true emergency, only action will serve you.

It is not irresponsible to let worry go. If you live somewhere that crime is high, lock your doors. Prepare, do your best and let go. Put your money somewhere you feel is safe, then trust it will be okay. Believe people are telling you the truth, unless you discover otherwise. Eat right, exercise and keep your stress down. Then go get a check up and have faith you are fine.

Perhaps you are afraid of people in general. Is it physical or emotional? How do you think they will hurt you? Will they steal from you? Will they speak against you? Will they try to cheat you? Are your feelings easily hurt by other's actions or words?

Trust of others begins with trust in our self. We must become secure inside our house of self if we are ever to trust other people. Many people today have come to lean upon their pets because they feel animals are very honest and direct. Although this is true, what we really love about our pets is that we can trust them to be consistent. Animals react in a generally consistent manner to how we treat them.

This is not bad, but, as human beings, we need to rebuild relationships with our own higher kind. Animals activate our compassion, our intuition and trust. We must learn to apply this to our own kind as well.

We all need safety in our worlds. Creating trust is imperative to building a safe world to live in. When we will not trust people outside of our own world, we limit our ability to trust and love. Fearful thinking can quickly poison a community to the point that it shuts down communication between its members. Violence in a community halts trust quickly, certainly. The fear of violence seizes it even more quickly. Consider how a community that suffers a loss through violence quickly comes together to mourn and heal. This is a response to the threat, love in action. Worry did not stop the act, nor did it heal it. Bringing hearts together to share what's left in love does. That's a far greater trust than we were willing to admit before any event took place.

Trust is a choice. So is fear. So is love. Each one carries its own weight. Love can certainly break your heart. Not just the romantic kind, either. Loving someone who ages and passes away hurts. Loving someone who comes into your life and leaves, for whatever reason, hurts. If you part on good terms, you will miss them. If you part on poor terms, you may harbor thoughts of unfinished business. Trust carries its own splendor and sadness. Sometimes trust is mislaid. Sometimes trust feels difficult when you can't foresee the future. However, trust is about knowing that all will be well, in the end.

This may be a tall order in your life. Trust that all is going to end well. There's no need to worry, no need for strife. Everything's fine. Even if you cannot see it right now, everything will be fine. Each moment that we choose to trust, we step into love. Fear brings us out of our loving walk, trust thrusts us back into it.

What do you worry about?
1.
2.
3.
4.
5.

Have any of the above ever happened to you? Circle it or them. Can you prepare so that you can safely say it will never, ever happen again? Mark your answers Y for yes and N for no.

List three things you can do to make sure each one marked Y doesn't happen again.
1.
2.
3.

For the ones marked N, why do you worry about it?
1.
2.
3.

If your five-year old self came to you and told you they couldn't sleep because of these things, what would you tell them?

If one of these things were to happen, what would be the worst result?

If you were shipwrecked and could only take three items,

name them:

1.

2.

3.

Are any of your worries (family, money, career) on your shipwreck list? Y/N

If the answer is Y, list five things you need to do to protect them so they can come with you to your island one day, if need be:

1

2.

3.

4.

5.

If they are not on your shipwreck list, consider why you worry over them. Are you worried about something very unlikely to happen? Do you worry to feel safe, knowing that it will make you feel exactly the opposite? Consider that you might actually worry just so you can ward off trouble of all sorts, but it's not realistic. Trouble may come your way, but remaining open, calm and prepared will ensure you can handle it in the moment with grace when, and if, the moment ever arises.

Trust that all is well and have peace in that knowledge.

# Make The Bucket List

Dare to dream. Dare to love. Dare to explore, to wander, and to finish.

You are not made of clay. You are made of blood and hope and dreams.

It is easy to become complacent. In your own mind, you can dream of a bigger life, a stronger outcome, or a fuller existence. But you must bring these into being through your body.

Possibly you assume that you should not desire too much, or hope too far. Your list of possibilities is small, and you don't want to ask for too much. Of course, it is noble to be humble, kind and generous. However, this life is for the giving and taking. Many of you solely give to your families, loved ones and even complete strangers, but you leave little or none for yourself. Why not dream here a little?

List three things you want to do:

1.

2.
3.

List five things that look fun but hard to do:
1.
2.
3.
4.
5.

List three things you have done that were very fun:
1.
2.
3.

List your best time ever:


List your best time ever by yourself:


If you could be five other people, who would they be?
Why?
1.
2.
3.
4.
5.

Name three silly childhood dreams (flying, riding a unicorn,
becoming a superhero):
1.
2.
3.

Name five things you must do before you die (leave nothing

out):
1.
2.
3.
4.
5.

If money were no object, name some things you would do:
1.
2.
3.

Who would you do them with?
1.
2.
3.

Perhaps it is easier to break it down by weeks, these ideas of yours. Many deeds can be done over a lifetime, but it takes today to get them started.

Name one, only one, bucket list item you could do, this very week, if you really wanted to:

What stops you from doing it?
1.
2.
3.

What are your fears?

Name the biggest:

Name the silliest:

Name the most likely to happen:

Name the thing you would regret most at the end of your life:

I didn't:

I was afraid to:

I blamed others for:

I was unwilling to let go of:

Making a bucket list serves two purposes. First, it puts down your innermost will on paper. These are your real feelings, your hopes, dreams, and desires. Second, it can tell you where you are off course. Perhaps your list is full of practical, daily to do lists, chores, grievances or tasks to be completed. The bucket list is meant to appeal to your higher power, a deep strength, and your thirst for adventure, wisdom and knowledge. Don't forget to add fun, as well. A list full of to do items can be an indicator that you need more time to yourself, perhaps a career change, or some self care. It is fine to not have glorious dreams of jumping a canyon on a motorbike or flying across the Pacific solo, but what's your equivalent? What about taking a class, seeing London, or learning to sew?

Think of ways to add tiny buckets to your list. Try a new place to eat, a new food, or some new dance steps. Find out the name of that beautiful tree you drive by, walk your dog in a new direction, or introduce yourself to your neighbor, even if you never have before. Perhaps you try a new color to wear, watch a travel program about a country you'd like to visit, or consider new magazines at the supermarket when you pass down that aisle.

Make your dreams come true, starting in small, meaningful ways.

Want to camel trek across Morocco? Why not try a horseback-riding lesson first? Want to live in the south of France? Try a French lesson online, bake homemade baguettes, or walk to a farmer's market this week. Feeling afraid to disrupt your life by getting a college degree? Take an online class first, buy a workbook on your subject, or find an app with quizzes. Small steps, taken one by one, create a path.

List ten things you must do before you die:
1.
2.
3.
4.
5.
6.
7.
8.
9.
10.

Choose one and circle it. Here is where you begin. Do not be afraid, you can do this. You deserve to do this. You very badly want to, right?

List one step to begin:

Name three websites or magazines or friends to get you started:
1.
2.
3.

What's your biggest fear?

List three ways others have gotten around that fear?
1.
2.
3.

Circle: Alone or With Someone

Circle: This Year or Next

Circle: I will be Different or The Same when I am done?

Breathe deeply. Do not worry, you are only dreaming, planning, hoping.

But, are you? This is your life. You, and everyone else, deserve great happiness. Your heart knows the way. Make the list, then cross item by item off as you complete. Put it somewhere you can see it easily, each and every day.

One by one, your dreams will come true. Believe. Don't give up and never doubt you can and will have your heart's desire.

# Who Do You Love?

Love is eternal, never ending and so very real. Why do we fight it so much?

The feeling of love has become associated with romantic partnerships, which, although wonderful, are not the sole way we can experience love. True love comes from not another, but from within us. In some ways, the act of being in love is simply a reflection of the beauty inside us already. We do not need another to experience love. We need to go inside.

Becoming love is something that we can achieve if we simply return to the presence of it already inside of us. It takes a willingness to open, to settle, and to gentle our self out of this busy world. Choosing love is simple, yet we avoid it most days. We have become accustomed to being right, being angry, being stressed. In the end, though, love is a choice.

What have you got to lose by loving more? Although you may feel vulnerable, you really haven't changed your position much. In fact, you have become stronger by rooting in something immutable and unfathomably deep in you. Your love is immovable, concrete, set in stone. No one can move you from this place of deep calm and peace. That is, unless, you let them do so.

Think of the people you love most. What would you do to defend them, protect them? What would you do to ensure that they thrived? How far would you go to make their progress possible?

Would you do these things for yourself? Do you place yourself last on your list of people to help? Do you stress yourself out trying to please people when what they really need is just your kindness and love?

Be gentle with yourself, and very honest. Do you share your beautiful love with the people you love most? Are you holding back, afraid to let go? Do you wait too long to tell people how you feel? Can you greet someone first or do you have to be invited to share a hug or handshake? Can you even look strangers in the eye anymore?

With love from within, you can do all of this from a place of grace. Relationships based in love flourish while ones based in fear rot from the inside out. Consider how you feel about your interactions each day. Do you fight with your spouse, your children, or your family? Do you enjoy your workplace? How about your interactions in traffic or the store or the drive through?

Imagine being in a red-hot love affair with someone. When you greet them at the door, do you hang back and wait for them to make the first move? Or do you immediately place your arms around their neck and go for the kiss, certain they will return your affections? This is what it means to be in love. Stepping forward with certainty that you will find a soft place to land, even if you jump from a high floor on the building. You are the soft landing, each and every time. With your love, you can ensure you will always come away from a situation the same as you came in, perfectly whole. By knowing that love is inside you, you can never have it stolen, corrupted or altered in any way. It is yours to keep forever. You can, of course, choose to turn away from it, but you are making a conscious choice to shift away from love when you react in fear, anger or any other negative feeling.

Why not be shameless about loving out loud? Who will it hurt? Certainly, some will resist by wanting to deny your loving attitude by choosing fear or judgment, but it does not need to affect you at all. Not a bit. You can just hang in love and relax knowing that you love yourself unconditionally. No one can take that away from you, either.

Even if you feel you can't love yourself unconditionally (yet), you can act in love with each step. Slowly, your love will pour into the cracks in your faith in yourself. You will be kinder to yourself; softer and more tolerant of what you once thought were grave errors. As you have positive interactions with others, you will begin to realize how a lack of love has shaped some of your less than perfect encounters beforehand.

Think about three times when you think love might have made a situation have a different outcome.
1.
2.
3.

Now think of a situation that really stinks right now:


How could love change this situation? Could you relax more, knowing nothing can be taken from you if you acted in love? Maybe you would create a solution you had never thought of, if you let go the fear of loss or rejection? Maybe you could see your opponent's side or another, hidden angle that you didn't see before?

Complete these sentences:

This situation could be different if I were willing to see love in place of:

I might see things different if I felt love when I looked at:

If I truly loved this person/situation like my best friend, could I begin to feel some love towards its resolution? Y/N

Think about the dialogue around this situation. If it feels awful, you may find you use language that makes it even more so. From a loving mindset, convert your statements from the negative to the positive.

If I really had to, I would say that the gift of this situation is:

In twenty years, the part I will laugh about is:

If I were the other party, I would see that the gift is:

If I were the most spiritual person on the planet, I would say: It's totally _____.

If your soul mate could find something good in this situation he/she would say:

You are wise beyond your years. No matter what your age,

you have the wisdom of love inside. Love acts like a wellspring of right action, right words, and right deeds when it is activated. Like a romance, living in love meets each moment in anticipation, peace and grace. You are perfectly present and prepared when you walk in love. Life flows as love goes. The obstacles that come along seem less dire, mountains less steep, people more kind.

Your inner landscape creates your outer reality. If you believe life is a struggle, it will be. Even in love, life will not be perfect or necessarily easy. However, you will be more prepared to meet your challenges upon the way as you walk in love. Chances are, you will see the ways you have been cruel to yourself and others before choosing to walk in love.

Just forgive yourself. It's in the past. Today, this very moment, is what matters most. The moments we have add up to lifetimes.

Name three times when you acted out of fear:
1.
2.
3.

Name three times you acted out of anger:
1.
2.
3.

Name five times you acted out of love in your lifetime. You had nothing to gain, maybe something to lose, but you did it anyway.
1.
2.
3.
4.

5.

Look over the lists. Which were easier choices? Chances are, sometimes the choices from love looked harder but a gut feeling told you it was "right." Pick one choice made from love, not fear, that you know would have ended up badly had you chosen otherwise.

Name it here:

Be still and have faith that you will make many more right decisions from love. Life is beautiful and ever changing, but with love, all things are possible.

# Why Do You Quit?

Let's get very honest. Why do you quit? Why do you give up so easily?

If you knew how very close you were to the finish line, you wouldn't quit so easily. Everything is so close, but you quit so early, you never see the fruits of all your waiting.

Your fear is telling you to quit, give up hope, and forget to dream. Don't listen to it. You are so close; it would be a shame to give up when you are already so close to winning.

Quitting is an act of killing faith. It not only gives up faith, it actively discourages it. When we give up waiting, wanting, being patient or even hoping, we kill off the part of us that believes we truly will have what we desire. We begin to question our trust that everything will be okay, the universe will deliver and we will be just as fine then as we are now.

It's very vulnerable to hope. In dreaming, we open our heart and let our minds loose onto our wish. When we don't see evidence of our desires, we begin to question the universe, our dreams and then, ourselves. We want to hope. That's part of how we are made. Faith is poured into each and every one of us at birth. We trust with the heart of a child, utterly and completely.

For some of us, faith slowly siphons off, as we grow older. Numbers, facts, and figures replace it. Proof is required to in all occasions to ratify the knowledge of the heart by the mind. Trust is given to that which can be seen, touched, felt or quantified. Faith is replaced by what can be seen by the eye or held in the hand. We relinquish our trust in the unknown and unknowable, isolating ourselves from the Divine because we can no longer see it. We forget all the times it has come through, our dreams have been made real, our visions for the future remarkably successful. We chalk it up to human intuition, or credit ourselves with great planning. We forget to credit that which we do not see.

We may have everyday faith, the type that pays a dire bill or saves us from oncoming traffic. That kind of faith we can handle more easily. We trick ourselves into believing that our actions are simply in line with the universe, instead of regarding our outcomes as something more divine, more holy. In our times, few would relinquish their daily outcomes to the Divine the way they do when faced with a major obstacle. It feels unnatural somehow.

Our disconnection has made the most natural of all acts, faith, to feel obscure, superstitious, or even mad. Is there really anything natural about worry or stress? If it were good for us, would our bodies respond the way that they do under times of disconnection?

Our natural state is wonder. Our brains crave excitement, our bodies are curious about this place, and our spirits seems to retain a sense of natural balance, even under extreme duress. We are quite resilient, even when we feel most down. When our dreams are coming slow to pass, we tend to quit our natural tendencies towards faith and slip into control mode. We do this by letting our mind run away with the ways we can't see our dreams realizing, counting up the unfair judgments and tossing out all the positive outcomes until we are treating our body, a spiritual machine, like a computer manufacturing lottery odds.

No wonder we quit. All evidence points to failure. Reason begs us to stay at the job, keep looking for more on the outside to fill the ache inside of us, or implores us to be "reasonable". Is there anything reasonable about love, about warmth, or the joy of sunlight? No, it is purely beautiful because we know what it means because of how it feels.

How does faith feel? What if we evaluate faith based on how informs our journey through this life? Let's begin with the most simple of faithful acts, believing it will all be OK. Maybe not today, maybe not tomorrow, or even next year, but knowing that somehow, somewhere, it's going to turn out all OK. If not, it's not over yet.

What stops your faith? Why do you quit?

List three reasons you quit:
1.
2.
3.

If you really wanted to, list three things you could do instead of quit:
1.
2.
3.

What is your biggest fear?

Name three smaller fears:
1.
2.
3.

If you had your dream today, what would be different? How would you feel? How would you act?

List five things that will be different when you have your dream:
1.
2.
3.
4.
5.

Are any of your fears tied to your results? Y/N

Name it here:

Think of three traits you think a successful person embodies. List them:
1.
2.
3.

Choose one:

Now list three teeny, tiny things you could do to be that person:
1.
2.
3.

Quitting midstream is common. Many people do it. At

some point, the bank of the river you have left is far behind, but the opposite shore is not yet in sight. You are in the middle where the current runs deep. You may feel as though there is no ground beneath you. You may feel like you are out luck, inspiration and talent.

Take one more step. Dare to dream on.

Name what got you started in the first place:

Now, consider your options. Are you willing to let all the work slide? You have completed the hard part: genesis. Whatever is lurking in the desk drawer, has been put on a shelf or lies hidden in your basement, you gave it life, even if only for a little while. Tender and newborn, it sits awaiting your return. How long will you wait?

The fact is the idea was a gift. You have received it, but not fully. Perhaps you questioned whether it was meant for you, or if it was meant to be at all. Be assured that it is. The universe does not make mistakes. It is, and always was, meant for you. Embrace it. Breath into it again. Let it live with your attention and dedication.

Let go of one fear. Just one will be enough to begin again.

Name it:

Write it down, burn it and bury the ashes. Know peace in letting it go.

# Make Time For Grace

When was the last time you stopped to smell the flowers-literally? When have you admired a bug for its iridescent wings or listened with true interest to your child's lament about the kids at school? How much have you missed being busy? When was the last time you sat down to pray on purpose?

We all waste precious moments being busy, but to what end? When you schedule time for grace, you schedule time for peace of mind. Doing that, however, may be harder than it seems. On the surface, it appears that we are doing it for no real ends. The effects of making time for grace in our lives transpires on the spiritual level, but may not be seen immediately on the physical plane.

We choose to forget that the world is in a state of perpetual grace and serenity. Every day, we must devote to connecting to spirit by choice.

Consider your day as it is now. Do you have a ritual, a time, or an action that brings you to the sweet spot of oneness with the world and more specifically, your place in it?

Do you pray? Journal? Meditate? Do yoga or go for a walk in solitude? Or perhaps you play music or paint? The point is, do something to make time to spend with your spirit.

In spending time with ourselves in grace, we connect to the universe as a whole. We spend time with the divine, and our minds ease on the earthly plane. On the opposite end, we can also choose to disconnect with our highest self and the world. We can eat too much, drink too much, or check out with too much paperwork, stress, worry and distraction. We avoid the love available to us because we are flat out scared of how miserable we are in some ways. So we check out instead of in, denying what needs to be fixed, let go of, and surrendered. It's an easy fix, but with big consequences.

List five ways you fall out of grace each day:
1.
2.
3.
4.
5.

Cross out two that could be eliminated.

Pick the one you think is the worst offender and circle it:

Now, let's turn it around. If you wanted to, how could it become something holy? If you love too much TV, could you pick programs to help you connect, like arts or science or public programming? Something that fills you with wonder, joy, beauty, and love while realigning you with your peace. Shift your focus to a different programming and the transition will be gentler.

If worry is at the top of your list, start by making list. List up to ten things you worry about each day. (Don't invent these if you only have only five items on your list).

1.
2.
3.
4.
5.
6.
7.
8.
9.
10.

Which ones are under your control and which are not? For example, if things like dying, world unrest and my neighbor's trees are keeping you up at night, that's God's domain. If things like, my weight, my work, my health, etc., are the culprits, those are in your domain.

Next to each entry, write a small m for things under your control, and a capital G for God's control (or D for Divine, U for Universe, C for Creator, whatever makes you comfortable).

Now, let's tackle some concerns with this simple prayer:

Dear God (Creator, Universe, Divine),

I worry too much. Please take my worries and handle them in your infinite wisdom. I know you will make it all OK.

Amen.

That's it.

Those things that cannot be changed are not your concern

anymore. You may only change the part you play in the world. You cannot change nations, history or even another's opinion. However, you can change yourself and the way you see the world.

Pray to change the way you respond to and handle situations and people. Pray to access the peace available to you each and every day, in each moment of every hour.
Pray all you want for your neighbor's dog, but that won't stop it from barking. Praying to not let it ruin your day will at least give you peace.

Finances got you down? Well, that's partly God and partly you. You respond in such a way as to co-create with the Divine on your behalf. As many people as deal with this issue, we should be learning to deal with it more effectively in this manner. As we think, we create. Worrying is creating exactly what we don't want to happen. Then we throw our cares to the universe when we are on the brink of disaster, begging for salvation or forgiveness or a little (or a lot) of both.

Why not do your best and let God worry over the rest?

By connecting everyday with the peace of the universe, we lay down our worries that caused us to try to disconnect in the first place. Maybe the reason we eat too much is because we are worrying over something that is God's problem, not ours. Maybe the reason we spend too much, drink too much, control other people or ignore cold, hard facts is because we are at a loss for answers.

This is when tuning in will bring us peace. First of all, we know that we are not alone. Second, something bigger, better, and unstoppable is on our side in this struggle. Third, and very important, we can hear the universe offer its whispered solutions. We can handle everything with some help.

Name three ways you think you might be able to connect to the Divine:
1.
2.
3.

Name three ways you know will never bring you closer to God, but others find transformative. These could include things you think are silly, ridiculous, boring or "just not you":

1.
2.
3.

Try three items from the above lists, even if just for five minutes, but include one item from the second list. (Note: don't try anything dumb, illegal or dangerous). This is an opportunity to do something new and integrate it into your daily life.

Five minutes of grace is better than nothing. Chances are, you will find that it grows and takes on a life of its own. What's important is that you connect, feel the peace and begin every day anew. Gain strength from being supported by a loving world that wants you to be happy and joyous.

It will never happen on accident. Make the time for the ever-present grace. Invite it into your world; realizing it was already a part of you, always.

# The Dream That Comes Back Wants You, Too

You have a calling in this life, and it wants you, too.

Nothing we do is by accident. Knowing this is important, because we must acknowledge our place in the world of things. Where is our center? Where is love? Where do we belong? These are questions that must take precedence in our thoughts, because it leads us to our true purpose in this world. Our purpose can heal ourselves as well as others, fills us with joy and love, and leaves this place just a little bit better than it was before we found it.

It doesn't matter if you are a banker, a baker, an engineer, an artist or a full time parent; your role is to live with love. A dream that returns to you, no matter how many times you turn it down, leave it behind, or outright forsake it wants you, too. It is likely you feel you have left something undone.

Energy in the universe is magnetic, but not to opposites. It draws unto itself its mate, its complement, and its completion. Whatever it is that you love, it loves you as well. Time spent in your calling feels effortless, natural, and somehow more right than any other person, place or thing in your life. Maybe you are gifted at it, or maybe you are not. It doesn't matter so long as you are passionate. There is a place for every gift, no matter how small or great.

Love reigns in the realm of spirit. Do not take lightly that which fills you with peace, joy and beauty. We are not our means, but our ends. Perhaps our employment is not necessarily our calling, but perhaps it could be. Maybe, if we let go, our passion could become a source of support financially. It certainly will become one emotionally and spiritually.

No matter how many times you might turn away from your dream, it will come back. Perhaps it's easy to see how it returns, like starting and stopping music lessons at different periods in your life. Or perhaps it's not clear yet, but you can't shake the notion that you should be somewhere, doing something. Listen closely and you will hear the answers. Whatever you do, the vague notion that you should be heeding an unanswered call will leave you with a vague sense of unease.

Make a list of five things you would do if you won the lottery in place of making a living:
1.
2.
3.
4.
5.

When you were five years old, what did you want to be when you grew up? In this world, we feel we must make a living of practical things. Perhaps, but we must also make the most of ourselves. Each of us has unique, wondrous, beautiful gifts to share. Some will share them with the world, others with a small circle of friends. The point is, one must become all that they truly are. There can be no holding back, because to do so would mean to restrict the flow of love. To do so means to be less alive, leaving us missing a part of ourselves.

It's no small thing to be what you love. It is not a matter of doing, but of embodying our love through our deeds. With speech, action and intention, we deliver our gifts to the world as a blessing to all we encounter. This is the stuff of miracles.

Do not be afraid you will fail, for you cannot if you act with great commitment. List five things you think might be a calling, a mission or a spiritual quest for you to accomplish:

1.
2.
3.
4.
5.


From above, choose the thing you would love to do but think might be too hard. Circle the item.

List three ways to make it easier to do:

1.
2.
3.

List three things you know will make it fail, ensuring your failure if you embark on it:

1.
2.
3.

Take note of anything on the second list that you might do to sabotage your success on the previous list. Have you been doing anything on this list?

What's the worst thing that could happen if you accomplished your dream?

1.

2.

3.

Face your fears here. It's okay to be cautious, but don't let fear rule your mind. If you want to play music in a band, why not start small? You don't have to quit your day job in order to follow a passion. Perhaps that would take all the pressure off to be perfect?

Breathe deeply. Close your eyes. See yourself at your happiest. What are you doing?

List three ways you could share that happiness:

1.

2.

3.

It could be as simple as a slide show of your travel photos to a senior center. It could be inviting neighbors over to learn how to make each other's favorite recipes. Or it could be blog about your passion, where you share and connect with people all over the world. It could be quietly sponsoring endangered animals or volunteering to feed the hungry. You could even run a social media feed for animals in shelters, increasing their chances of being adopted. Perhaps you could deliver your prize roses to unsuspecting neighbors. Maybe you coach a sport you love or become a part time tour guide of your hometown.

The point is it does not need to be a big deed. It does, however, need to be done with great love, as said by Mother

Teresa, "Not all of us can do great things. But we can do small things with great love."

Name three charities you'd like to sponsor, if you had the money:

1.
2.
3.

Could you donate your time? Become a volunteer or start a supportive venture that supports your causes? Be open to possibilities.

There is no reason your calling can't be lucrative. If you have an idea that serves your fellow man or animal or the environment, why not dedicate yourself to it full time?

Name five awesome jobs that you feel you could make a difference in:

1.
2.
3.
4.
5.

Investigate one this week. Do you need training? Could you start now? Could you try it out?

If it made you happy, truly, deeply, happy, could you find a way to make it happen, knowing that love outweighs fear? You have everything you need to accomplish it all, already inside of you. You just need to speak its name.

Dare to dream, because the dream wants you to call it in.

# Border Patrol:
# Expanding Your Lines

It's time to expand your boundaries. Who are you? Who do you think you are? Who could you be, if you let something unfold inside of you?

Can you imagine a different life, if you had to? Even if you are happy, you could still grow and change to become the sweetest, best version of yourself. Life is a never ending process of self discovery, enlightenment and growth opportunities, if you let it be.

If you let it be.

Life is wondrous in so many ways, but never more so exciting as when we are developing right before our own eyes. When every day presents a unique set of challenges that we can respond to with love, we are living at our best.

So many times, however, we let our fears stop us from growing. The unknown is so dark, so foreign, so unknowable that we can't even look at its face. All growth does not have to come from painful lessons or sorrowful events. We envision that all change is scary, but change can be very liberating and gently achieved, even when we face an unknown.

Imagine your life softer, gentler. Perhaps it's too soft, and it could use some roughing up, nothing too dangerous, but a good dash of spice.

Maybe you need to make some new friends, a new hobby, find a new job or relocate. Maybe you need to see that country you have always dreamed about. Or start that business. The point is, it doesn't have to be monumental on the outside to be monumental on the inside.

Imagine yourself doing your everyday routine with a twist. Start there. Could you add a new color to your wardrobe? What about music playing during dinner instead of TV? What about walking to work once a week (or take the bus)? How about talking to a stranger (an interesting and safe one, of course).

List five small changes that could add some spice to your life, if you wanted them to:

1.
2.
3.
4.
5.

Try one new idea every day this week. See how it feels.

Do not be afraid to grow. Life is about evolving, changing. You need growth, to, well, grow. It's tempting to want to grow while everything around you stays exactly as it is, but when you change inside, the world changes, too. It is not just how you see it. The energy changes, and you add new wisdom to the world. As you seek peace in this world through inner reflection, you transform your surroundings.

Do not give up so easily on the things and people that you love. Push against the barriers of your mind, simply by allowing a new reality to be possible. There is entire world out there calling you. It beckons, but cannot be heard if you don't listen.

There are people like you. Lonely? You don't have to be. For every interest, passion and plea, there are more like you. Even if you are an artist, a genius, a loner, or feel like an outcast, you can become connected to others who share your passion. Do not give up on relationships just because you haven't found your tribe, yet.

List three places you would hang out if you were you:
1.
2.
3.

Choose one and go hang out. Cruise around the block once or twice if you must. Take a brave friend. Take your dog along they are great conversation icebreakers. Just go.

You may find you have the time of your life.

You may also find you have more in common than you think. You may find that similarities are more common than differences.

List five people you don't like, don't get, or don't ever want to be:
1.
2.
3.
4.
5

Choose one you could stand, if you had to. You do, because he/she is now your cousin, for our purposes.

Name one thing you could like about them, if you had to:


Now another:


One last thing, even if it's their eye color:


Pretend you have an ark. You are saving the world from a flood. You must save the world's inhabitants, two by two. Only, they are opposites. Yin and Yang, Oil and Water, they do not mix or match. However, to make the world complete, you must include all.

Name three things you like about yourself:
1.
2.
3.

Now list their opposites:
1.
2.
3.

Perhaps you have overlooked a source of joy in this world because you see it as separate from yourself. Consider that the same is also true of them with your personality. If you were the opposite of your real self, could you see yourself as a whole, beautiful human being? Or would you pass judgment and move along to someone more comfortable, in your eyes?

Imagine for a moment that we all share the same source of life. What if, of only for a day, the world was connected by one big mind? And you, dear one, are but a cell in the brain? How would you view the others of the brain? Smarter? Richer? Thinner? Inferior? Not enough? How would you see them if you knew they were a part of yourself?

Unknown. You might very well choose to see them as simply unknown. After all, what would it hurt to investigate? Of course, don't do something dangerous, but be curious. Consider other's actions from a source of love, not fear.

List three traits you dislike in other people:
1.
2.
3.

Now give those traits to your dog (or cat, or snake, etc.). Imagine them acting out these traits in your house. You love them. See with love. What are they really doing?
1.
2.
3.

Expansion comes not from pushing outwards, but from dissolving the invisible fence on our hearts and minds to let the world in, bit by luscious bit. Do not give in to the fear that you are alone, untalented or somehow not enough. You know, in your heart, all you need to do is breathe, let go and be you out there in the world.

# Rinse. Repeat. Rinse.

Change takes time.

It also happens in an instant.

You never know where life will lead you, but if you prepare inside yourself, you will always find peace. True peace is never sought outside, but in the quiet recesses of the soul. This you should remember the next time the cat is missing. Or the dishes pile in the sink. Or your spouse blames you for global spinning, and the like. You have peace, right here, right now.

What really sets you off?
1.
2.
3.

Who is to blame?
1.
2.
3.

You are 100% responsible for your life. There is no one to blame. You can either change a situation, in which case you should, or you cannot change anything but your attitude. In either case, you are right.

Peace is right in front of you. Served up fresh everyday. You can possess it anytime you want. Loving contact is all that is needed to steady your ship in any storm. You only need to tap into its source.

All is well.

Name three things that make you feel at peace:
1.
2.
3.

Is there one can be done, anywhere, any time, any place? If so, circle it.

Inner peace and happiness comes from choosing peace and love on a daily basis. Although it may seem very difficult, especially if your life feels out of control or in turmoil, peace begins with you. The secret to growing from glimpses of serenity to a life of calm is to practice cultivation of it, every single day.

Peace cannot be found outside of one's self. Nor can it be found by searching. It is found by allowing peace in. It is right here, in front of each one of us, available at every moment. All we need do is recognize that it is, always was and always will be. When we step out of connection to our deepest calm, we feel it acutely.

Name five ways you step out of your calm, peaceful self:
1.
2.
3.
4.

5.

Choose one to eliminate from your life. Circle it.

Name three things you could do instead:
1.
2.
3.

Choose one to try out this week. Circle it.

Decide how you want to become an instrument of peace. Could you become calmer, sweeter, nicer, or even just not say anything if you want to be negative? Being right solves nothing, even if it seems important. Being kind will bring more to any situation than any amount of brain, brawn or righteousness.

The world needs love. It needs your love.

You may think that you need to get love more than you need to give it. Giving is getting. The love you need so badly can only be experienced by pouring it out on the world. This includes your loved ones, casual strangers and even people you do not necessarily like. They are really all the same. They are part of you, your world and your life.

As you become more loving, the world feels like it loves you back. For once, life gets easier, softer, gentler and more giving. Life flows as situations ease and things that seemed stuck forever change.

Everyday spent practicing walking in love will change how you see the world. It becomes less frightening, more inviting. Experiences are easier and the calm deepens inside of you as you begin to experience what walking in peace truly means. Other people's opinions, attitudes and problems affect you less. Of course, you still care. Of course, you still help the needy and serve others, but you bring a whole new level of peace to the encounter. Your stillness inspires, it delights, and it connects in deeper and more meaningful ways.

You are the peace you seek. Open your heart a little each day. Start today. Begin letting go of old hurts and grievances. You only hurt yourself holding on to anger, guilt, grief or revenge. Even if it seems justified, you are limiting your capacity for love and joy by living a life in emotional chains.

Letting go can feel messy, but remember you are getting what you give. Just give it a try.

Name five things you feel cannot forgive:
1.
2.
3.
4.
5.

Choose one you might be able to let go of, if you really, really had to:


Look at the words. Say silently, "I forgive. I forgive. I forgive."

Breathe in. Breathe out. Say, "I forgive you. I forgive you. I forgive you."

It is fine if you don't not feel it, or even mean it at first. Each day you practice, you will find it easier and more meaningful to say the words. Perhaps you will write a letter, or make a phone call, or un-harden your heart to the object of your grudge. Perhaps you need say nothing, simply knowing you have forgiven and moved on to love.

Every day, practice peace. Perhaps one day it will be easy, life will flow smoothly. The next, it may take hourly reminders to try to remain calm. This does not matter. What matters is that you begin to cultivate the knowledge that you can be peaceful by practicing each day to choose peace, practice forgiveness and walk in love.

It might not be easy. Or, it may be the easiest thing you have ever tried, to return your natural state of grace and joy. It is your right to be happy, but you must decide upon it. Insist upon it. It is your choice to remain miserable on this earth, or to step forward to something ultimately more rich and beautiful.

Life can spin hurricanes at you, throw mountains up where you once saw flat land, or blur your vision with complications not of your doing, but it is up to you, and you alone, to make a difference in your life.

Each day is an opportunity to begin anew. Do not let that chance pass you by because you are living in the past. Today is a new day, and it is the only day that truly matters, for you and for everyone else.

You are blessed. You are whole. Never forget that you are loved, each and every single day.

# If You Are Alive, You Are Not Done

Be quiet for a moment. Let the stillness take you. Sink into the quiet; let it envelop you.

See yourself in ten years. Where are you? What are you doing? How happy are you?

You are here to do something. Your past is behind you and you have a future to look forward to. Today is the beginning of that future. It is also your soon to be past.

If you do not like your past, now is the time to make a new one. Every new day brings an opportunity to put anything away and begin anew. Here is your chance.

You are not here to waste any of your precious time. Relaxing is not wasting, it is recharging. Pursuing is not wasting, it's belief in a dream. Wanting something other than what you've got is wasting energy in the wrong place. Bring the enthusiasm to your quest, your dream, your hope.

Let go of worry. Everything is in its place. Even if you have made mistakes, horrible and often, they need not hold you back from a brand new life. You can begin anew. It only takes the courage to step forth every day wanting to try,

Little by little, your now, your today will become your new past. A year from today you can be somewhere radically different than where you are at this moment.

Maybe you think you are too old, maybe too young, not smart enough, lack resources or education. That may be true on the surface, but not in your heart. You know you cannot blame your life on anything but a failure to try, and try with an open and believing heart.

Do not fear the external circumstances that surround you. They do not have to be true if you do not let them define your reality.

You may be broke in cash, but not in dreams, hope or integrity. You may be only one rejection away from the deal, the contract or the help you need to accomplish that dream that whispers to you endlessly when your mind is quiet.

List three traits you admire in older people:
1.
2.
3.

Which one would you like to possess? Circle it.

How would you develop that in yourself? Do you need training, practice or a different point of view?

Answer here:

Life is precious. Go forth and claim more experiences before you run out of time or energy or money.

Pretend you are about to retire (if you are older, pretend it's 25 year old you for this exercise). Now that you have finished a satisfying (or not) career, what do you want to do? Learn a hobby? Spend time with your family? Learn a language? Mentor someone? See the world? Write a blog? How about becoming a bartender in the sun? Work retail and meet lots of people? Help the elderly, disabled, homeless, or animal shelter? You can do anything, what will bring all your knowledge, joy and energy to people?

You are not doing it for anything but love.

List five occupations you could perform at no cost, but solely because you enjoy it. In fact, you would even pay to get to do:
1.
2.
3.
4.
5.

What would be most fun? Circle it. Now go do it.

There is no excuse to not be joyously working at something in your life. You deserve joy. You deserve to be happy, just like everyone else.

List three excuses why you can't do your "retirement" job:
1.
2.
3.

Circle the one you think is total baloney. Cross out the one you think could be dealt with.

If you had to, how could you eliminate number three?

Think you are too old to begin the road to happiness? Don't give up. You are not as old as you think you are. What if you live to love another 20 years? 30 years? What about 50? Who would you be? What do you want to do?

Many people live long lives of interest and wonder, well into their 80s and 90s. Do not believe because you are not young anymore that you cannot find a life of bliss that touches everyone you know.

It all begins with today. One step, one gesture, one decision can change your life forever for the better. You have the power to change lives. You simply must begin.

You have purpose here. You may or may not know it. It doesn't matter. You simply must be yourself, living to serve others with your gifts and talents. If you are still here, you have not lived out your soul's complete purpose. You are meant to do more in this world.

You are loved, believed in and guided. Follow that feeling of beauty to the place you know you have always been meant to be. It does not matter if you have wasted time before now. You simply get to make a different choice.

Perhaps you never envisioned yourself as you are today. You couldn't ever imagine the twists and turns your life would take. All is well, though. You are fine. You are strong. You can change it, if need be. You can trust that it is all turning out as planned in according the perfect unfolding of the universe.

If you saw a movie about your life, where the character had one last chance to be happy before dying, what would it be?

List five movie ideas with happy endings:
1.
2.
3.
4.
5.

Where is it set? Iowa? Italy? New York?  Deserted island?

Who is with you? Is there a leading lady/man? Best friend? Animal companion?

Who are you up against? Who is the antagonist?

What do you have to learn to win the battle or good (you) vs. evil (the situation, the company, the antagonist, etc.)?

Where does happily ever after occur?

When the credits roll, there is a picture of you. Underneath, it says where you are now.

Write your happy ending:

You are not finished. Your story is still being told. Breathe in and relax in that knowing.

## Notes

# Yesterday...
## Evaluate, Then Let It Go

The only reason to look over your shoulder towards your history is to learn. It is not to assign neither blame nor guilt, nor wish for other circumstances. Even your so-called mistakes hold immense value, if you choose to see your life in that light.

You never failed.

You never really quit. You are still here. You can begin again.

It's a beautiful life that lies before you. Go ahead and make the most of it.

List the single most important thing you have learned from your past:


How has it served you? List three ways:
1.
2.
3.

Think over your friend's mistakes, your family's mistakes. How did they help you grow?

1.

2.

3.

4.

5.

Lessons from our past are most valuable when they steer us clear of strife in the future. The problem is, there is no real future. There isn't even a past. There is only today, the beautiful, shining day that is right before us. Applying the lessons we learned from our previous experiences enables us to have happier, better futures by avoiding the repeat of unhappy situations.

Living in the past can make us bitter, solemn or cold. At best, it keeps our focus off the present moment by reliving our worst, and sometimes, our best moments. What about our moments to come?

List three shining moments from your past:

1.

2.

3.

Consider how these achievements might hold you back. Are you trying to repeat them? Are you resting on your laurels, not trying new things these days because your "best days" are behind you?

Do you have something that needs resolved? Something you need to resolve to heal, let go, and be happy? Be honest.

Name it here:


How would your life be different if you could forgive, forget and move on from this?

1.

2.

3.


List five people, places, or events you could forgive, if your really had to:

1.

2.

3.

4.

5.


What holds you back?


If it really meant that everything you want would come to you, in avalanches of beauty, success and love, could you do it? Could you let go and forgive?

Breathe in and out. You are whole. No one ever broke you. You are perfect.

You can forgive, because no one can ever hurt you. You are perfect in the eyes of the world, and you need not apologize for being you. Anyone or anything that tried to steal that from you can be forgotten, for they did not matter. Your soul is perfect, whole and pure. You only need to remember that.

In remembering, you can let go of all that has left you bereft, angry, jealous, bitter, feeling small or used, beat up or broken. You are perfect, just as you are.

List three things that you do to yourself to keep yourself hurting. Past hurts, old wounds, limiting beliefs and pleasing others all apply here. Tell the truth:
1.
2.
3.
4.
5.

Pick one you know is killing you. Circle it.

How does it serve you, protect you or keep you from daring to dream?


What would be different of you no longer did this or held this belief?


Does it affect how you relate to other people? How?
1.
2.
3.

What gifts has this brought you?
1.
2.
3.

If you could rewrite history, what three events, people or experiences would you omit?
1.
2.
3.

Since you cannot rewrite history, list how each "disaster" has brought you wisdom, knowledge, great people, or experiences you would have never sought out otherwise:

1.

2.

3.

4.

5.

The list can go on and on and on. You cannot escape your past. Assure yourself that you have been forgiven for all that you have done, even willingly. It is forgotten. The one who must now go forward is you.

Turn your face to the future. What lies behind you only serves to make you happy, now. You can glimpse how you were made by your experiences by looking at your past. Acknowledge the pain, the hurts, the triumphs but move forward into the now.

You are ever expanding, ever growing. The power of love in your life can outshine any horrible moment or act in your life. You are a beautiful being, just as you are. It does not matter what anyone thinks. Your life, your mind and your heart are yours alone.

As you face forward in your life to that which now awaits you, consider elements you would like to add. More love? More money? Better friends? More time? Less stress? Less stuff? More spirituality?

What do you need?

1.

2.

3.

The past is done and over. Now it's time to let go.

# Today
# Is For the Living

Today is the only real day you have. Not even today, but this very moment.

Isn't that beautiful? Bad or good, there it is. Here's a moment. Now it's gone. Here's another, now gone.

Take great peace in that reality. Nothing is ever as bad as it seems because, in a few moments, it will be over. The same is true for the greatest moments of life. They are over in a flash. Either way, the moments are like particles of dust in the light. Spinning and suspended, they float in the air unassisted. Neither good nor bad, they simply are as they are.

You can be that shaft of beautiful light. Imagine your particles of dust shining as you fill them with sunshine. It doesn't matter if they are dirt or diamonds you are the reason they shine.

Your life is a collection of moments, all strung together like party lights. Your memories, feelings and past are tiny portraits of your passing through this world. They are not who you are, they are experiences that you pass through. They need not dictate who you are or how happy you can become.

List five favorite moments:
1.
2.
3.
4.
5.

Now list five least favorite moments:
1.
2.
3.
4.
5.

Imagine reliving each one. Feel how it affects you emotionally, physically, and mentally. Notice how each one carries with it a full experience of the emotion of the moment in which it was lived.

The moment you choose to relive is the moment that you experience over and over again. Every time you relive an old moment, you are not living in the present moment. Of course, you could relive a happy moment like a marriage, a graduation or the birth of a child, which would bring you great joy, over and over.

Conversely, you could relive a less than happy moment over and over again. Perhaps you do not choose which moment, but are simply living in a barrage of unbidden memories that cause you alternatively joy and suffering.

Please pay attention. You are creating your life.

For example, think about high school. For some, this

brings back fond memories of camaraderie and joy. For others, it was a time of unrest and distrust.

How do you feel now that you have spent time reliving your moments?

Is it different from how you felt a few moments ago? Was it at all related to the rest of your day today? Did it cheer you, or did it make you sad?

Can you see how reliving past moments can change how you feel?

How do you feel right now?

And now?

How about now?

When you focus on just the moment before you, you may not feel much. You just are. That's the essential you. Just a being, having extraordinary experiences in this world, every moment, every day.

The world may come and go, but you are just the same every day. Your essential being is infallible, wise and unbroken. In the moment of now, untainted by other moments of past or future, you can see it just as it is.

Believe in yourself. Believe in your power to be perfect, just as you are. Take this special moment before you to realize everything is OK. You are OK. Life is OK. Everything is OK, just as it is.

Slow it all down, even for a moment. You have before you the chance to experience perfection, beauty and patience. It is all before you. You need not be, do, or reach to accomplish anything.

Many times we become unhappy because we try to do too much. There is no need to reach so far beyond one's self. The effort is not required, because you are fine just as you are.

If life were to end today, some of your dreams would remain untouched. Parts of your life would remain undone, unfinished. No matter how strong, brave, accomplished or intelligent you are, some things will be left undone when you pass. Your dreams are meant to lead you forward in life, developing you into a whole person full of love, experience, compassion and peace. It is the process of dreaming that brings you so much joy, which is why you begin anew every time one comes to fruition.

Your dreams do not make you miserable in their pursuit. Pushing your dreams to fill a hole created by the belief that you are not enough can, and very well, does make one miserable. Life is perfect, from beginning to end.

Begin each day believing that you are enough. You are perfect in every way. Your dreams are only a process of refining those traits you already possess. Do not let your pursuit of a dream interfere with your happiness.

This is not to say that you should not give your hopes and dreams your full attention. You may as well, because they will stay with you. Give them your full attention and pursue them with gusto each day. What cannot consume you is the struggle to make something happen on your timeline, nor the fear that you will not be complete without its fruition. Each day, strive to do your very best in your endeavors, and then let go of forcing it to happen.

Dreams are pulling you to a destiny. You need not worry so much about tomorrow, because only today can make a difference in your pursuit of dreams. Each day you step forward to that which is pulling you towards your dreams, you are fulfilling your destiny. It is the process, you see, not the result. One becomes a singer by singing, a dancer by dancing, a writer by writing. The song, the routine, the book, they are the result of being. They are the result of "doing" as well, but the doing is created by being first. A writer writes the book, but the book cannot make a writer. Do not worry so much about the result as much as the process to achieve it.

The beauty of a song is lived in listening to it sung, not in the singer who does not sing. It takes the present moment for her to make words in her mind, open her mouth and produce sound. In each moment, the song is created. Moment after moment after moment, until the song is over, the song is being sung. Certainly, she must prepare, study, memorize and practice and each of those deeds is performed in moments as well. The singer is still a singer, but never as much as when she is singing.

So it is with all deeds. Each day, deeds are undertaken that lead us in a direction. Far too many people suffer from stress caused by doing deeds that take them in a direction based on the fear that they are not enough, don't matter, or are not loved.

None of this is true. Every person is made perfectly. Suffering comes from trying to be someone else, somewhere else, anywhere but where they are. When a person steps into the present moment, all is settled. The present moment is soft, gentle; a place where each person can see that right now, they are enough. And that is enough for today.

# Tomorrow
# Is Tomorrow

Hope for the future begins today. Tomorrow is not for forgetting, but for remembering what we intended for today. Peace begins by remembering that all tomorrows are today's yesterdays.

They don't really matter at all. Days flow into one another in endless rivers of time. Tomorrow is the idea of another today. Certainly, plans are made, life plays out and lives are lived in a span of time. However, living in the vast unknown of tomorrow is reckless. It squanders today.

Tomorrow could be many things. What it will become is up to you to decide when you encounter it as it occurs. Hope is truly alive for tomorrow because you are dreaming it today.

Do not waste your life living in tomorrow. It doesn't exist. Neither does yesterday.

List three things you will do tomorrow:
1.
2.
3.

List five things you will do "someday":
1.
2.
3.
4.
5.

Circle one you could do today. What stops you from doing it today?

What one thing must you do before you die?

Name three reasons you haven't done it:
1.
2.
3.

Choose one to eliminate, today. Circle it.

Why must you do it? Name three reasons:
1.
2.
3.

Name three things you think will be bad if you do it:
1.
2.
3.

Name five things that will go right if you do it:
1.
2.
3.

4.

5.

Circle the number one reason in each list. Write them here:
Bad:
Right:

If today were your last day, what would you need to make it happen?

1.

2.

3.

Tomorrow can be used as an excuse to not complete things. Procrastination, based on authentic fear, can be a very real detriment to realizing one's dreams. Perhaps it is the fear of failure, or the fear of success, of not being enough or not deserving good in general, that holds people back from completing a task they truly feel compelled to do. Regardless, placing all the work in tomorrow's domain creates a never-ending timeline that results in delayed completion.

Consider something that felt like it took a long time to achieve or complete. For example, reaching adulthood, graduating college, getting married, retiring, etc. Think about the daily work it took to complete growing up, studying for the degree, going on dates, or building a retirement fund. Small steps built a reality everyday that eventually added up to a larger tomorrow.

Compare this with something you have been procrastinating about. How many days have you put off even the smallest action towards a goal or dream? Notice the resistance to doing even the smallest action towards that greater tomorrow.

That is fear at work.

Tiny movements can feel paralyzing. Small steps seem like giant leaps. Logical direction seems impossible or improbable.

The great news is it's not real. You can do this. You dreamt it. Now, believe in it. Believe in yourself.

What's your greatest fear?


How does it overcome your love of your dream on a daily basis?
1.
2.
3.

Consider your life is over. You look back. Give yourself some really good advice:
1.
2.
3.


Choose one of those advice items to put into practice, right now. This is your destiny. You must do this. You know deep in your heart what you were made to do on this planet. Now go do it.

You can do everything in your heart. That's why the dreams are put there. No one else's dreams are in your heart. Don't let their fear be in there, either.

You are enough. You are perfect. You can do it.

Tomorrow is but the product of today. Yesterday only serves us to learn, and the lessons are never ending. Each day that we grow, we have advanced in the direction of our dreams.

Never give up. It may seems like you are far away, but perhaps you are closer than you think. Today is the beginning of all the tomorrows you will ever have. So, begin at your beginning. There is no other way to start.

Name one thing you love about yourself:

Name one thing you have learned recently:

Name one thing you will do differently:

Be kind to yourself. Be true. Be real. Be well.

**Thank You**

www.ingramcontent.com/pod-product-compliance
Lightning Source LLC
LaVergne TN
LVHW051517080426
835509LV00017B/2092